New Zealand Fiction

Twayne's World Authors Series

TWAS 643

New Zealand Fiction

By Joseph and Johanna Jones

Twayne Publishers • Boston

New Zealand Fiction

Joseph and Johanna Jones

Book Production by Marne B. Sultz

Book Design by Barbara Anderson

Printed on permanent/durable acid-free
paper and bound in the United States of
America.

Library of Congress Cataloging in Publication Data

Jones, Joseph Jay, 1908–
  New Zealand fiction.

  (Twayne's world authors series ; TWAS 643)
  Bibliography: p. 94
  Includes index.
  1. New Zealand fiction—History and criticism.
I. Jones, Johanna. II. Title. III. Series.
PR9632.2.J6   1983   823'.009'9931   83-12662
ISBN 0-8057-6368-6

For our children: David, Judith, and Susan,
who shared our first visit to New Zealand thirty years ago

Contents

About the Authors

Joseph and Johanna Jones, both native Nebraskans, arrived in Austin, Texas, in 1935 as newlyweds. Dr. Jones at that time joined the English staff at the University of Texas where he is now Professor Emeritus. Mrs. Jones was a student at the university and later taught in the Austin schools in addition to writing book reviews. In 1953 a Fulbright assignment took the family, now numbering five, to New Zealand. Subsequently, they went to South Africa (1960–61) and Hong Kong (1965–66) where Professor Jones lectured.

He has contributed to various journals and edited *American Literary Manuscripts* (1960), *Image of Australia* (1962), and *WLWE Newsletter* (1962–70), together with upwards of fifty volumes for Twayne's World Authors Series, concerning authors from Australia, Canada, Africa, New Zealand, and the West Indies. His books include *The Cradle of Erewhon: Samuel Butler in New Zealand* (1959), *Terranglia: The Case for English as World-Literature* (1965), a small volume of poems entitled *Handful of Hong Kong* (1966), several similar volumes of "seventeener" (free-style haiku) poems of various dates, and *Radical Cousins: Nineteenth Century American & Australian Writers* (1976).

The Joneses have worked together in various library collections in England, Australia, and elsewhere for some fifteen years on what they call "World English." This volume on New Zealand fiction and two companion volumes on Canadian and Australian fiction (the latter in press) are among the fruits of this collaboration. Professor Jones, in retirement, has turned gradually toward nonacademic writing; *Life on Waller Creek,* published late in 1982, is a history of Austin and of the University of Texas as associated with a local stream, together with an inlay of personal reflections. Both continue to enjoy traveling, especially by ship, and hope to make several more voyages on whatever type of seagoing craft remains available.

Preface

New Zealanders have been publishing fiction for just over a hundred years—first as British immigrants and at length as native-born citizens. How does such writing differ from what has been done in Britain, or in North America, or at any rate in Australia? To begin, with, it was not intended to differ: the society that developed in New Zealand very much wanted to keep itself a faithful extension of that at "home"—merely a "brighter Britain" perhaps—but both time and distance worked against any such ideal. Early and late, there have been responses to a unique environment, one effectively isolated by distance during much of the national history. New Zealand writers have had their own pioneering and colonial experiences to chronicle, including a protracted series of Maori Wars. Fiction relating to the land itself began immediately to diverge, and more strictly social matters were slowly revealed to have evolved their own character, not always for the "brighter."

Though often thought of as somehow an extension of Australia, New Zealand is not actually very similar, either geographically or culturally, to its continental neighbor 1200 miles across the Tasman Sea. It was settled two generations later by the same European racial stock but not, proportionally, by the same social classes. Relative to area, its aboriginal inhabitants were far more numerous and able to resist to a greater degree the threat of extinction. In many areas, its terrain was more immediately suited to pastoral agriculture and for the most part has remained largely pastoral and highly productive. For some time now, however, the larger percentage of the population has lived in the cities—Auckland, Wellington, Christchurch, Dunedin—and in larger towns on the way to becoming small cities (for example, Nelson, Greymouth, Hamilton, Palmerston North). The thousand miles between the tips of the two major islands enclose in fact more than "just a small country" as it habitually likes to call itself; however, comparatively short distances between settlements (unlike Australia or Canada) helped to unify and consolidate local government and to promote cooperative state socialism of a moderate sort in a population tending naturally toward conservatism. As will be evident in much of the later fiction, this conservative local audience has not always been in tune with what New Zealand writers wished most to express: this fact, indeed, renders the country an interesting case study in a culture gap between writer and audience in addition to its long-familiar role of laboratory for social theory and practice.

As our study reveals, the early writers were nearly all pioneers first and writers only second (more often quite incidentally and briefly so). Before 1920 the record is sparse, for fiction as well as for other genres, but certainly not devoid of interesting talent. From that point to about 1950, fiction (along with poetry and literature generally) was consolidating itself and in retrospect, preparing for the appearance during the past twenty-five years of rapidly increasing numbers of professionally oriented writers, including Polynesians. This period also saw the founding of critical journals, improvements in local publishing, and the gradual emergence of a local audience more receptive than hitherto. All this has taken place within quite a limited population, still under 4 million.

This guide to the main tendencies and writers to be encountered in New Zealand fiction is arranged chronologically with some overlapping in the later chapters. Chapter 6, for example, deals with writers appearing since World War II; Chapter 7, "Persistencies," includes contemporaries but also some whose work began earlier. A summary account of the short story appears at the beginning of Chapter 7. The Chronology that follows gives main dates in New Zealand history together with some parallel dates for other parts of the Southwest Pacific; a number of authors and titles of fiction have been listed as well to suggest the appearance of new tendencies and/or important new authors. The Bibliography offers an introduction to the criticism of New Zealand fiction as well as a selection of background works in literature, history, and general culture. Some critical references to individual authors appear; these have been chosen with a view to their probable availability to readers as well as to their critical usefulness. The list of authors and titles is not intended to be exhaustive, but we hope it has not omitted very much that New Zealand critics would feel should have been included.

Our work on this study has been rendered easier and more pleasant by the library staffs at New Zealand House, Royal Commonwealth Society, and Commonwealth Institute in London; Alexander Turnbull

Library in Wellington; and the Grattan Collection of the Humanities Research Center in Austin. Dr. P. C. M. Alcock of Massey University, New Zealand, very kindly checked the Bibliography, adding several recent entries. Special thanks are due Suzanne Studdard for care and accuracy in typing the manuscript.

Joseph and Johanna Jones

Chronology

(Principal dates in Southwest Pacific and New Zealand history are given, together with other dates that relate especially to New Zealand fiction.)

c. 925   Legendary "discovery" of New Zealand by Polynesian navigator-hero Kupe.

c. 1350   Beginnings of Maori migration from northeastern Polynesia in long canoes.

1642   Tasman's discovery of western coast of New Zealand.

1769–1770   Cook's reconnaissance of both islands; de Surville's visit (Maori population estimated as about 200,000).

1773–1774   Cook's second visit.

1777   Cook's third visit.

1778   "First Fleet" of convict ships to Australia; Sydney founded.

1789   *Bounty* mutiny.

1791–1800   Visits by other European navigators (Vancouver, de Fresne, d'Entrecasteaux, Malaspina); beginnings of sealing, whaling, timber-cutting.

1797   Merino sheep introduced into Australia.

1809   "Boyd" massacre.

1814   Reverend Samuel Marsden (Whangaroa) establishes mission at Bay of Islands (by regulatory power assumed by Governor Macquarie, New South Wales).

1815   Birth of first white child in New Zealand.

1817   London government repudiates jurisdiction over New Zealand.

1819   Te Rauparaha active in Cook Strait.

1820   Hongi visits England; first use of Auckland harbor; earliest use of plow; first missionaries in Hawaii.

1821   Hongi begins conquest, using European arms; Lee completes Maori dictionary.

1823   Reverend Henry Williams and family begin residence at Bay of Islands; nonmilitary government in New South Wales.

1825–1826   First attempt (unsuccessful) at company-type colonization (Bay of Islands).

1832   Augustus Earle's *Narrative of a Residence in New Zealand.*

1833   James Busby arrives as British Resident; slavery abolished in British Empire.

1837–1839   Renewal of company-type colonization efforts; arrival of Baron de Thierry; formation of NZ Association (by E. G. Wakefield).

1840   Treaty of Waitangi; Wilkes discovers Antarctica.

1841   NZ becomes a crown colony under Governor Hobson; economic hardships in Australia-NZ, early 1840s.

1843   Wairau massacre: beginnings of Maori-Pakeha hostility; severe earthquake.

1845   Arrival of Governor George Grey (served 1845–53); E. J. Wakefield's *Adventure in New Zealand.*

1847   First "blackbirding" reported, Melanesia.

1848   Otago founded; Wellington earthquake.

1850   Canterbury founded; within next decade, European population surpasses Maori.

1851   Newspapers established at Lyttelton, Dunedin (South Island).

1853   Departure of Grey (who published *Poems, Traditions and Chants of the Maoris* same year); Maori "King Movement" begins (first Maori king in 1857).

1856   Colonial self-government achieved.

1857   Indian Mutiny.

1860   Maori Wars begin at Waitara (Taranaki).

1861   Gold discovery in Otago (preceded by lesser discoveries in the North Island, 1850s); American Civil War (threat of hostilities with Britain) begins; Henry Butler Stoney's *Taranaki* (first NZ novel).

1862   First telegraph line (Lyttelton-Christchurch); Mrs. J. E. Aylmer's *Distant Homes.*

1863   First steam railway (Ferrymead-Christchurch); Samuel Butler's *A First Year in Canterbury Settlement;* Frederick E. Maning's *Old New Zealand.*

1869   Julius Vogel treasurer ("Vogelism": borrowing and public works through 1870s); University of Otago founded; rabbits (introduced 1867) reported as pests.

1870   Christchurch-Dunedin railway line.

1871   Lady Mary Anne Barker's *A Christmas Cake.*

1872   End of Maori Wars; Samuel Butler's *Erewhon.*

1873   University of Canterbury founded.

1879   Adult male suffrage.

1880   Auckland Free Public Library.

1882   Refrigerated transport for meat; Fine Arts Association (Wellington), University of Auckland founded.

1886   Eruption of Mt. Tarawera.

1888   Full depression (extending into 1890s), with people leaving NZ; electric lights (Wellington).

1889   Julius Vogel's *Anno Domini 2000.*

1891   George Chamier's *Philosopher Dick.*

1892   NZ Academy gallery opened.

1893   Women given franchise.

1897   U.S. annexation of Hawaii; Victoria University of Wellington founded.

1898   Old Age Pensions Act.

1899   First troops to South African War (1899–1902).

1901   Cook Islands annexed; Federation of Australia; Samuel Butler's *Erewhon Revisited;* Alfred A. Grace's *Tales of a Dying Race.*

(Comparative population figures at beginning of twentieth century in millions [total world population, 1,488]: China 350, India 294, Russia 146, U.S.A. 80, Germany 56.3, Japan 45.4, Britain 41.4, Indonesia

37, Canada 5.3, Australia 3.7, New Zealand .816—
North and South Island populations approximately
equal.)

1904　First Rhodes scholarship awarded; Arthur H. Adams's *Tussock Land.*

1905　"All Blacks" (rugby team) christened.

1907　Dominion status conferred.

1908　Workers Compensation Act; completion of Auckland-Wellington railway.

1911　Widows' Pension Act; wireless installed.

1912　Blanche E. Baughan's *Brown Bread from a Colonial Oven.*

1913　Waterfront strike.

1914　William Satchell's *The Greenstone Door.*

1914–1918　World War I: capture of West Samoa; troops to Egypt, Gallipoli; conscription introduced, 1916; troops to Western Front.

1918　Katherine Mansfield's *Prelude.*

1920　Railway strike; West Samoa mandated to NZ; Anzac Day officially perpetuated; Jane Mander's *The Story of a New Zealand River.*

1925　Broadcasting service begins.

1926　Census reveals slight majority of urban over rural population; Massey University founded; Jean Devanny's *The Butcher Shop.*

1928　Kingsford-Smith flies across Tasman Sea.

1929　Murchison-Karamea earthquake; beginnings of world Depression.

1931　Statute of Westminster (charter of British Commonwealth).

1932　Depression riots (Auckland, Wellington, Dunedin); various relief measures enacted, early 1930s; Nelle M. Scanlan's *Pencarrow.*

1934　Air transport service begun; trans-Tasman airmail inaugurated; John A. Lee's *Children of the Poor.*

1935　John Guthrie's *The Little Country.*

1936	Compulsory unionism established; inter-island air service begun; Margaret Escott's *Show Down;* Frank Sargeson's *Conversation with My Uncle.*
1937	Ngaio Marsh's *Vintage Murder.*
1939	*New Zealand Listener* founded; John Mulgan's *Man Alone.*
1939–1945	World War II: declaration of war against Japan, 1941; fall of Singapore and compulsory enrollment for military service, 1942; Canberra Pact and mutual-aid agreement with Canada, 1944.
1942	Roderick Finlayson's *Sweet Beulah Land.*
1947	*Landfall* founded; State Literary Fund established; National Orchestra founded.
1948	Eruption of Mt. Ngauruhoe; David Ballantyne's *The Cunninghams.*
1949	Daniel Davin's *Roads from Home.*
1950	Controversy with Britain over dairy prices; troops to Korea.
1951	ANZUS treaty; waterfront strike broken by emergency regulations; Frank S. Anthony and Francis Jackson's *Me and Gus.*
1952	NZ Players founded.
1953	Ascent of Mt. Everest; coronation of Elizabeth II and royal visit; Tangiwai rail disaster.
1954	SEATO treaty; James Courage's *The Young Have Secrets.*
1956	Colombo Plan conference in Wellington.
1957	Maurice Duggan's *Immanuel's Land;* Janet Frame's *Owls Do Cry.*
1958	Sylvia Ashton-Warner's *Spinster;* Ian Cross's *The God Boy.*
1959	International Antarctic treaty; Errol Brathwaite's *Fear in the Night;* Maurice Shadbolt's *The New Zealanders.*
1960	Noel Hilliard's *Maori Girl.*
1961–1962	Alarm over British negotiations with Common Market; minister to EEC appointed.

1962   Visit by king and queen of Thailand.

1963   Visit by Japanese prime minister; New Zealand House (London) opened; Bill Pearson's *Coal Flat*.

1964   Ronald Hugh Morrieson's *Came a Hot Friday*.

1965   Troops to Vietnam; trade agreement with Australia; Graham Billing's *Forbush and the Penguins*.

1966   Visit by U.S. President Johnson.

1967   Decimalization of currency and devaluation of NZ dollar; Renato Amato's *The Full Circle of the Travelling Cuckoo*.

1968   *Wahine* (interisland ferry) disaster.

1970   Royal visit and visits by Prime Minister Trudeau (Canada) and Vice President Agnew (U.S.); All Blacks to South Africa; James McNeish's *Mackenzie*.

1971   Luxembourg agreement (giving NZ adjustment period with EEC on dairy products); Race Relations Bill; first annual conference, New Zealand Maori Artists and Writers Society.

1972   Continuing economic controversy over wages-prices; Witi Ohimaera's *Pounamu Pounamu*.

1973   Springbok (South African) rugby tour of NZ banned; frigate sent to observe (protest) French nuclear tests at Mururoa Atoll; Albert Wendt's *Sons for the Return Home*.

1974   Visit by shah of Iran; NZ dollar devalued.

1975   Muldoon (National Party) ministry comes to power; broadcasting corporation restructured, separating radio and TV.

1976   Economic austerity policy invoked against growing inflation, unemployment (highest since 1930s); All Blacks' tour of South Africa protested by numerous withdrawals from summer Olympics (Montreal).

1977   Visit of Queen Elizabeth II (Silver Jubilee tour); sharp political controversies.

1978   National Party wins general election; continued economic instability; Maurice Gee's *Plumb*.

1979   Further inflation; 24-hour general strike.

1980   Recombination of broadcasting agencies; expulsion of Soviet Ambassador Sofinsky; continued political and economic difficulties; significant migration of population to Australia and elsewhere.

1981   Controversy over South African rugby team in NZ.

1982   Legal restrictions on NZ citizenship for West Samoans; partition of Micronesia into republics, federations, etc., largely completed; harsh drought in the South Island.

(Comparative population figures for late 1970s, in millions [total world population, 4,321]: China 958, India 637, U.S.S.R. 258, U.S.A. 220, Indonesia 143, Japan 114, Germany, East and West, 78, Britain 55, Canada 23, Australia 14, New Zealand 3.11)

Chapter One
Sheep Kings, Cockies, Maoris, Miners

At Tuapika we found an excellent inn, and a very good dinner. In spite of the weather I went round the town, and visited the Athenaeum or reading room. In all these towns are libraries, and the books are strongly bound and well thumbed. Carlyle, Macaulay, and Dickens are certainly better known to small communities in New Zealand than they are to similar congregations of men and women at home.

—Anthony Trollope, 1873

Interviewer: It is generally agreed that New Zealand has not produced a single notable author, poet or dramatist who has achieved success by remaining in his or her native land. Is there, in your opinion, any reason, apart from limitation of experience and narrowness of viewpoint, why this should be so?

Mr. Shaw: Any man who follows a profession is more or less bound to follow his market. As a matter of fact New Zealand is not a literary centre. But England and London and Paris are literary centres and you really have to follow your market to a certain extent. That is the only thing to do if New Zealand is to develop this. I did not know that New Zealand had not produced a single notable author or poet or dramatist. Perhaps it may congratulate itself upon that—it is a very questionable occupation.

—George Bernard Shaw (interview in New Zealand, March 15, 1934)

The Setting: New Zealand

After one walks down some easy steps onto the grass-green carpet of New Zealand's exhibit (we are at the Commonwealth Institute on Kensington High Street, London), one encounters a more or less circular area some forty to fifty feet in diameter, filled with the sort of pictorial and statistical information that any skillful publicity effort would furnish. There is, for example, a model airliner poised over a panorama of the Southern Alps, bleak and rugged enough in contrast to the lush dairying and meat-growing farms in the other murals. We are cautioned, however, that "New Zealand is not just a gigantic farm—Only one worker in eight is in agriculture—The country has a factory to every half-dozen farms." Notwithstanding, the eye is drawn quickly to a "mechanical cow" of plastic, wire, and metal. This apparition lights up and clicks, illustrating its physiology, as its milk squirts into a receiving pail. Symbolic? Yes—certainly of the intense mechanization and careful monitoring of the product for export, which is a far cry from the helter-skelter farming with which the incoming hordes of Pakeha (non-Maori) settlers began dispossessing the Maoris after the 1840s. Symbolic in some other ways, too, as what we are to learn about New Zealand fiction will suggest.

Farther along, a diorama shows a logging operation, with accompanying pictures of pulp and paper manufacture and samples of eight common woods, all except two (radiata pine and Sutherland beech) bearing Maori names, among which *kauri* is easily the king, *rimu* perhaps the most useful and common. Other graphic exhibits give us views of alluvial flats or extensive plains, thermal areas (especially in the North Island), coasts (with beaches and rugged shores), mountains, glaciers, lakes, rivers in abundance. Photographs and old prints contrast three of the principal cities (Wellington, Auckland, Christchurch) today with their beginnings in the 1850s. There is a small plaster statue of Captain James Cook, charts and dividers in hand, with a color portrait of Cook in a lighted panel (this time holding a spyglass in his hand). Maori artifacts (feather cloak, hei-tiki of greenstone, or nephrite, and the like) are overshadowed by some fine specimens of intricate dark-wood (probably totara) carving inlaid with *paua* shell, their shapes and techniques related to other Polynesian cultures far to the north and east.

As we come nearly full circle, we may pause to look at a carefully composed model of "Farmland in Taranaki" (southwestern North Island) backed by a painted panorama of Mount Egmont, a symmetric snow-covered volcanic cone as perfectly formed as Fujiyama. A labeled diagram in front of the model picks out the bush (rendered realistically to show differences between eucalypts, tree ferns, cabbage palms, and macrocarpa), farmhouse, dairy herd, milking shed, water supplies, shearing shed, spray dip (for sheep), electric line with metal oppossum shields on the poles, dog kennel (for four), and airstrip. Opposite, a revolving photographic drum reminds us of many scientific, technological, and sociopolitical facts: that the telephoto lens was invented in the 1880s by a New Zealand geologist; that seeding from airplanes was first tried there in 1906; that Ernest Rutherford first split the atom in the 1890s and demonstrated transmission of radio waves in 1894; that Samuel Duncan Parnell, a carpenter in Kokoroko, first insisted on an eight-hour day in 1840 and thus established the "8 Hours Movement"; that on March 31, 1903, a backcountry South Island farmer named Richard William Pearse flew a monoplane somewhere between 450 and 600 feet (nine months before the Wright brothers) but kept no recorded proofs of his accomplishment; that—perhaps in an effort to forget some of all this—New Zealand ranks second or third among the world's largest per capita consumers of beer; that the use of solar energy there dates back to 1950; and that New Zealanders were pioneers in pasture ecology, stamp-vending machines (and printed advertisements on the backs of stamps), racehorse breeding, dairy cooperatives, gold dredging, municipal milk supply, and road-safety patrols for schools. Portraits of people (color transparencies) emphasize the diversities among a population now somewhat over 3 million, living in an area larger than the British Isles which most New Zealanders have finally (not long ago) ceased to call home.

Just above this exhibit we have been visiting, tucked in among many others and below still more (the entire large hall is much like a world's fair in miniature), is the institute's pleasantly arranged library and resource center, which contains quite a good cross section of New Zealand writing. One of the novels to be found there is *Mackenzie,* by James McNeish, published in 1970, two centuries after Cook's rediscovery (following Tasman's brief sail-by visit in 1642). It is a book of broad dimensions, set in the province of Canterbury (South Island) during the 1860s, a time when the Maori Wars were raging in the North Island (explored in Brathwaite's recent trilogy of novels) but the newly arrived southerners were possessing the land and founding fortunes by wool growing and gold mining, both arduous and risky pursuits. History and myth are blended in *Mackenzie,* as are idealism and avarice, gentility and savagery. Published almost a hundred years after Samuel Butler's *Erewhon* (1872), it is a book of intention and dimension worthy to be compared with such a predecessor. One of its principal characters, the gentleman sheep farmer Amos Polson, is in fact rather a Samuel Butlerish figure in a number of ways: he plays classical music on a piano which he has transported to his sheep station; he is a religious skeptic and wide-ranging philosopher, a friend of important people in Christchurch but by nature

a solitary (he is a widower, with a grown daughter), much given to
speculation about what is to follow the period of discovery that he is
living in. But whereas *Erewhon* begins in a search for more sheep pasture and finds hidden among the Southern Alps a cloud-cuckoo uto-
pia, *Mackenzie* (in which the fierce commercial urge for more sheep
pasture is not neglected) returns the reader—assisted by a hallucinogenic drug from the native *tutu* bush—to the vision of a Miltonic
"womb of nature and perhaps her grave" as Mackenzie, his dog, and
the remnant of a flock of sheep arrive at a mystical tree surrounded
by age-old cairns of rock.

This divided book appropriately represents for us, at the outset, a
divided country—or should we say a divided world—and is conveniently available for representation in the literary art of a small but in-
tensively productive country. In *Contemporary Novelists* (1976), a bio-
critical reference containing about six hundred names of novelists
from the English-speaking world, New Zealand is represented by the
same number of novelists, just under twenty, as nearby Australia
whose population is over four times as great. The lists appended to
the present study are naturally more comprehensive than this, but the
reader may see, from the large number of writers represented by no
more than one or two titles, how difficult an extended literary career
has been and often still is in this small and distant land.

Emigration Fiction

Certainly it was never the intention of the first settlers in New
Zealand to set up a new center for the writing and publication of literature in English. They came because they chose to, not because
they were compelled to, as were the earliest Australians; yet some of
them felt that events in Europe were such as to make emigration far
more desirable than remaining at home. They began to come a half
century later than Australians had, and were a much more homoge-
neous and more highly "cultured" group. The dreamers among them,
of which there were not a few, dreamed not of escape, of ease from
degradation and brutality, but of an establishment, a rational and
easy transformation of their new homeland into a purified and—to a
degree—democratized "brighter Britain" at the Antipodes. Numbers
of the wealthier newcomers were able to acquire (usually by lease)
large enough tracts of land to set themselves up as owner-operators of
sheep stations—"squatters"—especially on the South Island. These
people became, economically speaking, the aristocrats; but there were

also artisans and small farmers of humble station and limited re-
sources. Dairy farmers came to be known as "cow-cockies"—cocka-
too-farmers, suggesting that all they could raise on their land was
cockatoos, which were already there (the term probably originated in
Australia, from where settlers, miners, and land speculators came, as
well as directly from Britain).

Given this situation—settlement by generally literate, orderly,
law-abiding people, some of them bona fide intellectuals, in physi-
cally demanding but comparatively predictable surroundings—what
is the earliest time one would expect some kind of deliberately literary response to begin to appear? Five years, fifteen, or at least a generation? If we set the date of "earliest settlement" at 1850, we will
not be too far out of line, though of course there were a few traders,
missionaries, and other miscellaneous settlers before that time; the
pioneering elite, if that term is descriptive of any set of genuine pioneers. On this basis, the record is not too disappointing: highly
readable prose narrative of distinct individuality (Frederick E. Maning's *Old New Zealand*) by 1863, and before another decade, one of
the world's satiric masterpieces (*Erewhon*, 1872, already mentioned).
These are peaks, of course, but they do exist and may be legitimately
accounted as part of New Zealand literature. What, then, of the
foothills, vales, and gullies?

Systematically promoted immigration, such as developed quickly
after New Zealand had been annexed and opened to protected settlement in the early 1840s, produced a "literature" of its own, the largest part of which is strictly utilitarian, but with a smaller part
half-utilitarian, half-creative. This can be observed in the earliest
writings pertaining to North America as well as to Australia and Africa. Here is an example of the first type, from *Chambers's Papers for
the People,* 1870, #85:

In the first place, the emigrant should educate himself for the object he
has in view. A little knowledge of European languages, of mathematics, of
land-surveying, of mechanics, architecture, geology, botany, chemistry and
veterinary surgery will be most useful to those who desire to attain superior
success. More practical accomplishments, however, will suffice for those of
the humbler order. . . . Arrived in New Zealand, listen to no grumblers,
and be careful how you accept the services of strangers. Waste no time in
the towns, but proceed at once to the scene of your future labors. There, if
the choice of situation be tolerably prudent, industry, frugality, and thrift
will certainly bring independence and fortune in their train.[1]

Fiction written with similarly utilitarian ideas in mind, or partly
so, is often interesting to historians and social critics, though it receives (and no doubt deserves) less attention from literary historians.
In this chapter, a few examples will be given space, and other authors
and titles mentioned, out of a genre that is surprisingly extensive and
long-lived as well. A century and more after the first titles appeared,
novels were still being published whose main aim seems to have been
explaining "what it's like Down Under."

The earliest travelogue-promotional novel, Mrs. J. E. Aylmer's
Distant Homes; or the Graham Family in New Zealand (1862) missed by
one year a chance to be counted officially the "first" New Zealand
novel. This honor goes to Major Stoney's *Taranaki: A Tale of the War*,
published in Auckland in 1861 (perhaps a "travelogue" novel too, if
we recall the British soldier's occupation at this time as one likely to
send him to very nearly any part of the world). Published in London
and evidently intended for a home audience, *Distant Homes* is mostly
autobiography thinly papered over, with every intention of creating
the best impression possible. In retrospect, a great deal can be
gleaned from such a passage as the following, which describes a meet-
ing with a group of South Island Maoris:

> The day before this feast, Captain Graham had received a colonial news-
> paper with an account of the war, and felt very anxious to hear what the
> natives would say.
> First the chief of the tribe who had come as guests stood up, and, a space
> being cleared, he began brandishing his spear, and running backwards and
> forwards, shouting out his speech all the time, and, when excited, springing
> high off the ground. He spoke very eloquently and beautifully, bringing in
> all sorts of natural objects to illustrate his meaning, and comparing the
> Queen to the sun, the Governor to the moon, and the English to the soft
> winds, that, passing over the earth, made everything good rejoice. He was
> not what is called a missionary native, that is, a converted one, so did not
> make use of scriptural names and types, which the other chief did, when he
> stood up. In speaking of the war, they both said it was wrong, and, if they
> fought, they would fight for the good English, and the more English came
> the better as they brought raiment and riches with them, and all the lis-
> teners expressed their approval, so that there appeared no cause for appre-
> hension in that quarter.[2]

In the final chapter, news comes that son Tom has been appointed to
serve in the Royal Navy (as he wished). At this, "Poor Mrs. Graham

could scarcely believe it possible, and did not know how sufficiently to express her thanks to God for this mark of his kindness and mercy."[3]

A neighbor of Samuel Butler's in Canterbury, Lady Mary Anne Barker, published in the 1870s several books of her reminiscences of station life, one of which, *A Christmas Cake in Four Quarters* (1871), took fictional form. *Station Life in New Zealand* (1870), the best known of these, is notable for skilled reportage which comes very near at times to then current fictional methods. Like Butler's *First Year*, it is based on personal letters. Davin's *New Zealand Short Stories* reprints, from *A Christmas Cake*, "Christmas Day in New Zealand" from which this portion of a shepherd's yarn is taken:

"Well, of course I meant to ask and to hear all about it, but I thought it would keep until we had had a bit of dinner, for it was about two o'clock, and you must please to remember, ma'am, that we had breakfasted some-where about five, and likewise that walking up and down them back ranges is hungry work at the best of times, besides being wearing to the boots. 'Where's Davis?' was my first words. 'Davis must have gone away altogether for a bit,' they said, 'for the hut is locked and fastened up until it can't be fastened no more, and unless we reg'larly break into it, we shall never get in it.'

" 'Drat the fellow!' I cried, 'there ain't no bushrangers about. Why doesn't he just lock his door and hang the key on a nail outside where any-body can see it, as I used to do when I was a back-country shepherd, and wanted to go away for a bit.' But it was no manner of use pitching into Davis, not then, because you see, ma'am, he wasn't there to hear himself abused, though we did that same and no mistake. It *was* aggravating—now, ma'am wasn't it? There was we three, and the dogs, poor things! as hungry as hungry could be; and we knew there'd be flour and tea and sugar, and likely a bit of bacon (for Davis was a good hand at curing a ham of a wild pig), inside the door, if we could only open it."

A decade later, Alexander Bathgate's *Waitaruna* (1881, also pub-lished in London) reveals a society that has already reached, or per-haps merely resumed, stability. Such books, however, were still being regularly subtitled "a story of New Zealand," "a story of New Zealand life," or "a story of colonial life," indicating that for the home audience, novelty had not yet worn off. This was to continue for most of the remainder of the century and indeed beyond that. A few titles will illustrate: W. H. G. Kingston, *Waihoura, or the New Zealand Girl*, 1873; W. M. Baines, *The Narrative of Edward Crewe*,

or Life in New Zealand, 1874; William Langton, *Mark Anderson, a
Tale of Station Life in New Zealand*, 1890; Dugald Ferguson, *Bush
Life*, 1893; John Bell, *In the Shadow of the Bush*, 1899; Edith Searle
Grossmann, *The Heart of the Bush*, 1910. Of these, all except Lang-
ton's were published in London.

Gold-mining yarns by Henry
Lapham (*We Four*, 1880) and Vincent Pyke (*The Story of Wild Will
Enderby*, 1873, and a sequel, *The Adventures of George Washington
Pratt: A Story of the New Zealand Goldfields*, 1874) are also typical, and
their analogues continued to appear in the novels of such twentieth-
century writers as Will Lawson and Ruth Park. Behind these literary
(or semiliterary) descriptions and narratives, it is well to remember,
lies a great body of travel writing and chronicling of early explora-
tion, often illustrated by artists in such ways as to reveal contemporary attitudes toward primitive man and his scenic surroundings.
Such a study as Bernard Smith's *European Vision and the South Pacific,
1768–1850* has a good deal to tell the literary student as well as the
art historian. A much later novel, Henrietta Mason's *Fool's Gold*
(1960), is based on diaries of the gold rush days.

The Maoris

The sort of quasi-vaudeville performance described by Mrs. Aylmer
is not altogether different from what appears in *Old New Zealand*
(1863), a semifictional account published under the pen name, A
Pakeha Maori, otherwise Frederic E. Maning (1811–1883). Maning
was born at Dublin and came to Tasmania with his parents at age
twelve. Ten years later, he took up permanent residence in New Zealand, for some years as Pakeha Maori—a term applied to white traders who lived among the Maoris and often as not intermarried with
them. He had the confidence of the natives in one of the many tribes
in the thickly populated northern tip of the North Island, above
where Auckland stands today. After his career as trader, he engaged
in sawmilling and in 1865 was appointed judge of the Native Land
Court, serving until retirement in 1876. Although many writers
from Captain Cook onwards had something to say about the Maoris,
none managed to say it with quite the same entertaining mixture of
gusto and sympathy that Maning brought to the writing of *Old New
Zealand*. A shrewd humorist, he understood the value of using himself as the butt of the joke, and at the same time, he wanted his readers to understand how Maori society functioned and what a curious

mixture it presented with its system of *tapu* (taboo) and other customs, its warlike yet chivalrous intertribal relations, its good humor
and tolerance within its own rigidities. Maning concludes his third
chapter with these ironical reflections on contemporary writing and
the events it describes:

> Now if there is one thing I hate more than another it is the raw-head-
> and-bloody-bones style of writing, and in these random reminiscences I shall
> avoid all particular mention of battles, massacres, and onslaughts, except
> there be something particularly characteristic of my friend the Maori in
> them. As for mere hacking and hewing, there has been enough of that to be
> had in Europe, Asia, and America of late, and very well described, too, by
> numerous "own correspondents." If I should have to fight a single combat
> or two just to please the ladies, I shall do my best not to get killed, and
> hereby promise not to kill anyone myself if I possibly can help it. I, how-
> ever, hope to be excused for the last two or three pages, as it was necessary
> to point out that in the good old times, if one's own head was not sufficient,
> it was quite practicable to get another. . . .
>   Hail, lovely peace, daughter of heaven! Meek-eyed inventor of Armstrong
> guns and Enfield rifles; you of the liquid fireshell, hail! Shooter at bull's-
> eyes, trainer of battalions, killer of wooden Frenchmen, hail! (A bit of fine
> writing does one good.) Nestling under thy wing, I will scrape sharp the
> point of my spear with *pipi* shell; I will carry fernroot into my *pa* [fortified
> village]; I will *cure* those heads which I have killed in war, or they will spoil
> and "won't fetch nothing": for these are thy arts, O peace![4]

When we move forward to the turn of the century, to a collection
of stories by Alfred A. Grace, *Tales of a Dying Race* (1901, London)
we could very nearly ascertain from this single book what happened
in the distant (North Island) war the Graham family were hearing
about forty years earlier. The supposedly "dying" race quite obviously
had lost the war, but some of the stories testify to the heroic account
they gave of themselves against the most powerful nation in the
world. The preface speaks of the Maoris' love of fighting, which the
coming of the Pakeha only made more fierce and bloody—with guns
instead of spears and stone axes. It also states that eleven of the total
of twenty-eight stories first appeared in the Sydney *Bulletin* (whereas
only two appeared in the New Zealand *Triad* and one in the Dunedin
Star, the only New Zealand journals mentioned). The collection thus
reflects the *Bulletin's* preference for short, crisp narrative.

In addition to the tales of warfare, there are others revealing much
about Maori-Pakeha relationships. "Arehuta's Baptism" relates how

a Maori woman, resisting Christianization of her tribe by a German missionary (the story offers examples of fractured English), takes her child on her back and swims out to sea to drown. "The Blind Eye of the Law" recognizes a white man's marriage to a Maori woman who owns ten thousand acres of land, over the claim of Ruku, her exhusband. In "Why Castelard Took to the Blanket," a white man goes native for the love of a Maori girl. In a love story with still another angle, "The Tohunga and the Taniwha," a manufactured *taniwha* (fearsome water monster), concocted by sailors from a trading schooner, saves the beauteous Miromiro from marriage to the *tohunga,* an old priest-artisan whose name, Tuatara (a species of ancient lizard), signifies how ugly he was. This is a comic tale; others include "Te Wiria's Potatoes," "Big Piha and Little Piha," and "The School-Ma'am and the Mormon Elder." There are other "monster" stories as well and tragic ones like "Horomona," in addition to "Arehuta's Baptism" already mentioned.

Grace's narrative art is sentimental and "elegant" in the mode required by the period during which he wrote, but at least it is an advance on one of the early novels quoted by the critic E. H. McCormick, in which a Maori witch is made to say, "I have here a decoction of the poroporo *(solanum lacincatum),* which will heal thy wounds."[5] Among a sizable number of other writers who imagined they were elegizing a dying race or recalling their now-vanished fierceness were G. H. Wilson, *Ena, or the Ancient Maori,* 1874; John White, *Te Rou; or, The Maori at Home,* 1874; R. H. Chapman, *Mihawhenua,* 1888; H. B. M. Watson, *The Web of the Spider,* 1891; and "Rolf Boldrewood" (from Australia), *War to the Knife, or Tangata Maori,* 1899.

Seeking to explain why such fiction about Maoris is "virtually unreadable," Professor Joan Stevens says—sympathetically—that the writer had very little tradition to guide him in presenting primitive life: Cooper and Melville, perhaps, and who else?

And then the world he was attempting to portray was so *totally* unfamiliar—its landscape, its people, its history, its customs; even the motives for action could not be taken for granted. And how to render speech?
As a result, Maori novels, if they are serious, tend to sink beneath the weight of explanation. The purely exploiting, entertaining novelist can pluck out the colourful titbits he needs and skim the rest; however wildly improbable his yarn, there will be readers to swallow it. But the truthful imaginative artist who is drawn to fiction with a basis in the past of the Maori people faces a task of enormous complexity.[6]

Of the titles mentioned above, John White's *Te Rou* has the most serious intention of trying to represent reality.

At a still later stage of development, the Maori story (which as we shall see is still very much alive in New Zealand literature) grew to the stature of a serious novel in the hands of William Satchell (1860–1942), who published *The Greenstone Door* in 1914 (a very poor year to launch a book, as it turned out). Satchell was born in London where, before emigrating to New Zealand in 1886, he had briefly begun a literary career. Settling in the Hokianga district north of Auckland, he attempted farming but was unable to make a living on the land, then became a storekeeper, and finally moved to Auckland, where he and his large family encountered varying fortunes. He was a journalist and clerical worker and for a short time published his own one-man literary journal, the weekly *Maorilander*. Commencing as a New Zealand poet, he turned in his middle years to fiction. In spite of what he must have recognized as literary failure, Satchell liked to think of New Zealand as offering "a good rousing chest-opening life among equals."

Satchell's method in his two Hokianga novels, *The Land of the Lost* (1902) and *The Toll of the Bush* (1905), is to introduce into pioneer culture

. . . a man from the outside world, well-educated or of good social standing, who loses his status in the eyes of petty, conventional frontier society. He falls in love with the daughter of a leader of the community, but is temporarily frustrated because he is not valued at his true worth.[7]

"Petty, conventional frontier society"—the phrase is Phillip Wilson's, himself a novelist—is one to conjure with, for in one guise or another it will be appearing through most of the remainder of this account of New Zealand fiction.

The Greenstone Door is pro-Maori, though as Wilson says, its picture of old Maori *pa* life, based on such good studies as *The Maori Race* by Edward Tregear, is "highly colored."[8] Between the Hokianga novels and this one, Satchell had published *The Elixir of Life* (1907), a shipwreck-and-desert-island romance with philosophical overtones; so it is not surprising to be told that in *The Greenstone Door*, he had "got down in his thinking and his art to the basic essence of all human activity, so that the ambitious moral tone of his colonial community is seen to reflect that of society in general."[9]

J. C. Reid concludes that while Satchell has a good many faults, a lack of narrative power is not among them:

His books do continue to excite the reader, and to convey an impression of vitality and authenticity. [Thus,] for all the criticisms that may be made of it, [with *The Greenstone Door*] the novel in this country begins to be a New Zealand novel, and take its first tottering steps alone.[10]

There were problems to be faced in New Zealand society that had not yet fully emerged as serious ones; and Satchell, well fitted by experience to speak for the misfit, the outcast, helped to bring such problems forward.

Other early novels using Maoris as principal or important characters include Jessie Weston's *Ko Meri* (1890), H. B. Vogel's *A Maori Maid* (1898), Bannerman Kaye's *Haromi* (1900), and A. H. Adams's *Tussock Land* (1904). *Ko Meri* is set in Auckland with as much glitter as Auckland society of the day has to offer, which is quite a little: teas, dances, concerts, Christmas parties, and so forth. A half-caste Maori princess, Mary Balmain, who has been made into a lady by her guardian, attracts a young English soldier and they are married. He is killed in battle, however, and she returns to her "own people" to "share the darkness" with them, since, as everyone knows, they are a dying race (except that they weren't, as it proved). *A Maori Maid* has as its heroine another half-caste, Ngaia, actually an heiress but not known to be so until the denouement. She marries a young Englishman, whose father is a nobleman, and they go off prospecting for gold until all is revealed at the right time. *Tussock Land* is set in the South Island where yet a third Maori half-caste girl of nineteen, Aroha Grey, falls in love with a young Pakeha, King Southern of Dunedin (a New Zealander this time, not an Englishman). Social pressures being what they are, he cannot bring himself to accept her, but after a flight to Sydney he returns and they are united. Adams sees Aroha as the stronger one, the truer New Zealander, and King as a member of the actual "dying race." The ending, says Joan Stevens, implying that racial and cultural blending is the only solution for the future of New Zealand, "was highly unorthodox in 1904, though it may yet be the verdict of history."[11]

This chapter, in Maning's phrase, has been very much in the fictional tradition of *old* New Zealand. The writers of fiction over the better part of a century were interested chiefly in using—exploiting— the colonial situation after one fashion or another: to explain to the home audience what pioneering life at the Antipodes was "really like"; to show the Maoris in a warlike, romantic, or even comic light as the case might be; to display the scenery to advantage and even to use it as the backdrop to satiric fiction; to present, at length, the improved social scene as evidence of how well the project of transplanting European culture had worked out. Apart from racial conflict— seemingly destined to resolve itself through convenient if pathetic disappearance of the defeated Maoris—there were few if any serious problems raised by most of the writers. Alexander Bathgate's self-deprecating statement in his preface to *Waitarunga* might serve as a kind of summation for much of the whole period: his pictures, he says, "have been strung together, as it were, by a story, not very interesting in itself, perhaps, to the ordinary run of novel readers, but one which it is hoped will help to a better knowledge of life in the colony."

Chapter Two
Utopia and Vice Versa

I am there now, as I write: I fancy that I can see the downs, the huts, the plain, and the river-bed—that torrent pathway of desolation, with its distant roar of waters. Oh, wonderful! wonderful! so lonely and so solemn.

—Samuel Butler, *Erewhon*, 1872

With the dawn of the year 2000, the world has become convinced: "First. That labour or work of some kind was the only condition of general happiness. Second. That every human being was entitled to a certain proportion of the world's good things. Third. That, as the capacity of machinery and the population of the world increased production, the theory of the need of labour could not be realized unless with a corresponding increase of the wants of mankind. . . ." Thus, on the eve of the nineties, were foreshadowed the principles of its social legislation, in fact of future New Zealand democracy.

—E. H. McCormick, 1959

In most parts of New Zealand, nature is not so intractable as in Australia or Africa. Settlers found that the land yielded plentifully if taken care of, and a general mood of confidence, especially following the Maori Wars of the 1860s, was enough to convince Englishmen-becoming-New Zealanders that with enough hard work virtually anything could be achieved. Their political leaders encouraged them in such beliefs. Beginning with Butler's *Erewhon,* the closing years of the nineteenth century saw an interesting cluster of utopian and anti-utopian books published by New Zealanders (either marginally so or permanent citizens). Such books reflected at times the social and political theories the writers themselves held and evidently found an audience for; at other times, skepticism or satire was the aim. There was, moreover, a strong current coming from overseas—from the Marxists and other socialists in Europe, from Bellamy, George, and others in North America, and from Australia. All this in time gave support to reformist groups whose proponents were not necessarily utopians but shared at least the belief in trying hard for betterment in a still flexible society as they viewed it.

The Utopians

In 1889, Julius Vogel—prime minister of New Zealand from 1873 to 1887 (with interruptions) and father of H. B. Vogel, author of *A Maori Maid*—published a prophetic novel with the title *Anno Domini 2000; or Woman's Destiny*. (Bellamy's *Looking Backward*, which inspired a number of congeners—not necessarily Vogel's but he could hardly have escaped knowing about it—appeared in 1888.) Never one to propose doing things by halves, Vogel lays out a program for Great Britain which includes repossessing portions of the United States (by force), instituting a program of Social Security, giving Home Rule to Ireland, and providing strict equality between men and women. The latter accomplishment is not altogether surprising, since all this wonder-working has come about through the marriage of Hilda Fitzherbert, duchess of New Zealand, to the British emperor, her new position affording remarkable opportunities for the practice of statecraft. As for the usual technological advances to be found in utopian fiction of that time, people rise in "air-cruisers" (of course), telephone one another with ease, and use their expertise to enrich themselves further. On the Molyneux River, an old gold-fields favorite, which is conveniently drained for inspection, gold is discovered in such quantities and such pure state that five-thousand-ounce boxes are filled to capacity by the hundreds. All this belongs to Hilda and her sister Maud who show "feelings of quickened, vivid emotion," but: "It is only justice to them to say that their feelings were not in the nature of a sense of personal gratification so much as one of ecstatic pleasure at the visions of the enormous power for good which this wealth would place in their hands."[1]

At the end of his book, countering the argument that "natives of countries where the earth is prolific are not, as a rule, industrious," Vogel argues that these are the very countries to which "the higher aims which grow in the path of civilisation have not penetrated." Once such penetration has taken place, presumably:

An incalculable increase of wealth, position, and authority would accompany an ameliorated condition of the proletariat, so that the scope of ambition would be proportionately enlarged. There would still be much variety of human woe and joy; and though the lowest rung of the ladder would not descend to the present abysmal depth of destitution and degradation, the intensely comprehensive line of the poet would continue as monumental as ever,—

"The meanest hind in misery's sad train still looks beneath him."[2]

As E. H. McCormick's epigraph to this chapter (taken from an account of Vogel's novel) suggests, a fair amount of what Vogel had to say was already destined for political action in the New Zealand parliament.

A few years after Vogel's book came Edward Tregear's *Hedged with Divinities* (1895), a reversal of Empress Hilda's position through a cataclysmic plague which kills all the males in the world but one, Jack Wallace, who is besieged by females and finally elected king of the women of New Zealand. The office carries such arduous polyandrous duties, however, that the king—who cannot logically abdicate—is obliged to flee. (A twentieth-century novel, James Ray's *The Scene Is Changed,* 1932, has a similar plot.)

Two books by Professor J. McMillan Brown, writing as Godfrey Sweven (*sweven* is Anglo-Saxon for "dream"), consider both sides of the case. *Riallaro* (1901) sends its hero cruising among various islands with symbolic names—such "ugly coinages [the New Zealand critic Miss E. M. Smith thinks them] as Meddla, the Isle of Philanthopy, Palindicia, the island where justice was always being dealt out, and Swoonarie, where wild-cat schemes were always being foisted upon the people."[3] *Limanora* (1903), much longer and cloudier, is somewhat more in the *Looking Backward* tradition. Miss Smith believes that the influence of Samuel Butler is to be "plainly seen" in Brown's volumes, though as to *Riallaro,* at least, a better case might be made for Herman Melville's *Mardi.*

A passage from *Limanora* introducing a discussion of eugenics will serve to illustrate Brown's style as well as perhaps point (dimly enough) toward such later writers as Huxley and Orwell:

It was indeed a period of accelerated progress, if not of precipitance, in the work of all families. The darkness around existence lifted over the whole horizon, and demanded redoubled exertion, in order that the new regions should be mapped before it fell. The tissues and nerves of every Limanoran felt the stimulus; each worked with a will. Still the necessities of the situation almost ran ahead of their powers. One thing became clear, that they must have more workers; the new generation would have to be more numerous than the last. For the young had to be drawn upon for active nerve- and head-work before their usual time; and these would need more leisure in the next stage of their life to compensate for the loss of it in the period of growth.

It grew evident that parents who had been exceptionally successful in the two children they had brought forth, reared, and launched full-fledged on the career of life should be permitted and stimulated to resume parentage. It was considered one of the highest privileges and honours to be selected as parents again by the magnetic consciousness of the nation. There was needed no formal agreement of resolution; the mind of the race was known without consulting it openly; and every pair felt in a moment that they were selected for reparentage; they required no stimulation, no permission to enter on the patriotic duty. And all considered it a duty of the loftiest kind. Passion in the race burned low; no longer was it a sting or goad that had to be mastered; it was in short no more a passion, such as the use of imagination, the love of the race, or the yearning after advance had become. The animal element in it had grown insignificant, and left it at the bidding of intellect and will. These . . . parents had thus no sensuous pleasure to seek in the new task. . . . They took it upon them as a duty, and their chief pleasure lay in the honour they had been paid, and in the service they were doing to the race and to the progress of their humanity.[4]

Both for style and for ideological impact, it is instructive to compare this passage with Chapter 19 of *Erewhon,* "The World of the Unborn."

Anti-Utopia: Samuel Butler

Having looked at Butler's successors (whether his deliberate followers or not), we come back to *Erewhon* as the one survivor out of the lot. Before publishing *Erewhon* (1872), Butler (or his family on his behalf) had already published *A First Year in Canterbury Settlement* (1863), put together from his letters home. This he tried later to disown, possibly because it was received with mild ridicule in New Zealand. He was already preparing himself for *Erewhon,* however, as *A First Year* to a degree itself shows in its accounts of exploring and living in the Southern Alps. The opening chapters of the satire are deceptively unsatirical; they read like carefully selected parts of an explorer's journal, organized into a continuous narrative. (There are many such in early New Zealand writing, some of them quite well done; and they have come in later times to be used by novelists and storywriters as source material.) Not until the seeker (for new "country," new grazing areas for sheep, since unoccupied territory was already becoming scarce) has gone up a new pass and crossed the divide do we become aware that we are in utopia-upside-down, with a none-too-well-defined plot line but with whole chapters of witty satire the like of which had not been seen for a long time.

Erewhon is so well known (or alternatively, if the reader has not yet encountered it, his pleasure and surprise should not be dimmed by too much comment here) that quotation or extended reference seems unnecessary. It is, of course, not New Zealand society per se that Butler is dissecting; what was there had been so recently transplanted that even pioneering behavior had not yet become clearly defined. In the South Island especially, and Christchurch above all, British ladies and gentlemen were fulfilling an imperial mandate by residing in a colony where they took every pain to preserve the closest possible connections with "home." Butler's contributions to the local Christchurch *Press*—the kind of urbane essay writing done by not a few of his New Zealand contemporaries, who like him were readers, thinkers, and musicians—were enough to set him going and keep him at his task of surveying Victorian institutions; and his short but sufficient exile at the Antipodes lent added perspective. The question of whether he was New Zealander enough to qualify *Erewhon* for a place in New Zealand fiction is conclusively answered in the opening chapters.

Observers and Reformers

We have seen, then, in Butler, Vogel, Brown, and one or two others a small lively whirlpool of utopianism and its antithesis, remarkable enough when we remember the time and place that brought it forth. When we come to look at reform writing, a genre that the age was producing in great quantities in most parts of the English-speaking world at the time the "Canterbury Pilgrims" and others came to New Zealand, we do not encounter anything so entertainingly written. Two major themes—women's rights and temperance—were to be found, sometimes interlinked, and most of the books were by women in the approximately thirty-year span between 1890 and 1920.

Pioneering women often assume leadership and are accorded consideration more readily than their sisters and cousins in the metropolis or other part of the mother country, almost as if to acknowledge that strong and faithful wives and mothers are essential to survival. A good many of the earliest New Zealand men, moreover, were of a type ready to concede that denials of justice did indeed lie behind the half-century and more of campaigning with varying degrees of militancy. New Zealand was a new place, possibly even *the* new place, the one outpost whose situation could be thought providential; therefore, it was all the more urgent to drive hard at the old wrongs.

Among the women writers were Louisa Baker, with *A Daughter of the King* (1894), Constance Clyde, *A Pagan's Love* (1905), and Edith Searle Grossman with several titles including *A Knight of the Holy Ghost* (1907, in which an Australian heroine fights brutal opposition) and *The Heart of the Bush* (1910, set in South Canterbury). Writers of temperance fiction (which included a few men) were equally numerous: A. A. Fraser, *Raromi* (1888), Alice Kacem, *For Father's Sake* (1887), Kathleen Inglewood, *Patmos* (1905), Susie Mactier, *The Hills of Hauraki* (1908), Guy Thornton, *The Wowser* (1916, about a "wowser" parson, at a time when prohibition was beginning to seem a possibility), and H. Foston, *At the Front* (1921). There is no doubt that drunkenness and ensuing brutality of all descriptions were facts, with grim effects on women and children together with men, but fiction did not rise to art in dealing with them; the books were journalistic, propagandistic at most, despite the valid problems they attacked. Some, no doubt, were intended to generate or influence legislation, of which there was a great deal that explored avenues of social relief.

So far we have met writers who present positive ideas in very positive ways: they are satirical about what they dislike, enthusiastic about their schemes of social paradises to come, or indignant about social abuses as they see them. In the final book to be considered, George Chamier's *A South-Sea Siren* (1895), attitudes are lower-keyed, resembling more closely the country-house or dinner-party situations to be found in such contemporaries as W. H. Mallock, William Dean Howells, or Henry James. It is in effect a sequel to an earlier work, *Philosopher Dick* (1891), using as a principal character Richard Raleigh and some of his friends. The small community of Sunnydown has its social strata and is preoccupied with morals, social attitudes, and the importance of material possessions; but it can also rise to the consideration of universal education, the understanding of current religious and scientific theories, and broad views about the meaning of life. There are structural affinities with eighteenth-century fiction, such as digression and symbolic character names. Symposia take place in the Growlery, Richard Raleigh's bachelor den; meanwhile, the "siren," Mrs. Wylde, touches the lives of many prominent men in Sunnydown. Emotional, wily, self-centered, having few if any female friends, she manages her admirers so skillfully that she and her husband, Commodore Wylde, entertain and live lavishly without funds of their own for many years. The Seymour family, in contrast, are genuinely cultured. The father, widowed, has two grown daughters of whom the older (for novels of this period, an unsentimental, frank heroine) is a refreshing balance to the siren even though—like colonial girls generally, being in short supply—she is much sought after. But to return briefly to the Growlery, here is a sample of the talk:

"Then, again, I look at the question in this way. If wealth brings happiness it must follow, as a rule, that rich men should be happy. Now, I happen to have known several rich people intimately, and I have been brought into contact with many more, and I can honestly say that a more niggardly, grasping, soured, discontented, and miserable set I have never met anywhere. They can't enjoy their money when they have got it."

"Then they can give it away, and afford relief and employment to others."

"But that is just what they don't do."

"Well, I know what I should do with it. I could find many ways of enjoying it."

"No doubt,
                         And so say all of us;
but then, my dear fellow, *we shall never get the chance!*"[5]

Before leaving the first part of this study, in which we have explored a rather scanty but certainly not altogether barren record of early fiction, it may be worthwhile to pause long enough to look at the territory ahead in order to gauge in some degree the rate of growth. One may gain an idea of how long New Zealand literature lacked any significant volume of production in fiction by consulting a chronology-bibliography, *A Century of New Zealand Novels 1861–1960,* by James A. S. Burns. Here are the statistics, bearing in mind that quantity and quality are very different matters, that one *Erewhon* is more than a match for a dozen volumes like *Limanora* or *Distant Homes.* From 1861 to 1930—two generations—we find that one (or none) to three novels a year is the regular pattern, with only these years as exceptions: 1874 (seven titles), 1896 (five), 1899 (four), 1905 (four), and 1926 (five). After 1930, including World War II, no year shows fewer than three titles and most years more; then, beginning with 1950, there is quite a sharp rise: the ten years, 1951 to 1960, yield a total of ninety-one, or an average of just over nine per year, but no year until 1957 shows more than ten. From 1961 to 1970, the figures both for single years and the yearly average would be a good deal higher.

We must expect, then, that the second part, which takes us to 1945, will almost certainly be more richly textured and somewhat more populated with writers, but the full impact of the twentieth century did not reach the younger literatures like that of New Zealand until after the end of World War II. (This century has been far and away the most prolific for English writing that we have yet seen: when we measure it against the total past of what the language has produced, we will be surprised.)

Chapter Three
Expatriates

It was not that either Katherine Mansfield or Frances Hodgkins totally lacked leisure, paper, pens and paint in New Zealand; on the contrary, each added to her impediments and poverty by going away. They did lack, however, an environment in which they could hope to work themselves to the full. They were conscious of great talents, and convinced that those talents would be stifled in a country that was still, in their eyes, raw, colonial and antagonistic. Whatever was the objective truth of their assessment of New Zealand society, their subjective accuracy cannot be questioned.

—W. H. Oliver, 1960

It was Jane Mander's generation, already adult before the Great War, who saw with bewildered dismay that the country now offered its young less than they themselves had had, and much less than they had imagined themselves working to provide.

—Dorothea Turner, 1976

Long before the phrase *brain-drain* had been coined, New Zealand was experiencing the phenomenon it described. The country is so much aware of long-continued expatriation that the entry "Expatriates" in the fine *Encyclopedia of New Zealand* (1966) runs to just over thirty pages, studded with snapshot biographies under thirteen categories which display pride mingled with regret. Explaining why the problem of expatriation is implicit in the New Zealand situation, the authors point out the isolation, small size, and surplus of certain kinds of talent in a yet-emergent land. "The attitudes of the early settlers," moreover, are those of "many of their living descendants,"

. . . and this is particularly true of the arts and of pure scholarship: in a considerable number of New Zealand minds they are regarded as trimmings, fair enough as far as they go, but not to be compared with a hydro-electric dam or the manufacture, under license, of a new type of gentlemen's underwear. This is a perfectly natural point of view and the wonder of it is that there should be so many New Zealanders who hold to a different set of values.[1]

Since the lists in this article are confined to living writers, some of the most prominent names are absent; they include Hector Bolitho (only minimally a writer of New Zealand fiction), James Courage, Daniel Davin (both of them important New Zealand novelists), Dorothy Eden (principally a writer of suspense novels), and Ruth Park (whose output has been divided between New Zealand and Australia). To these names must be added those of Katherine Mansfield (the earliest and generally best-known of all), Jane Mander, and Robin Hyde. Among notable literary expatriates, it can be seen from this, the women outnumber the men.

Katherine Mansfield, one of New Zealand's most accomplished self-exiles, grew up in Wellington as Kathleen Beauchamp in a home of more than average comfort and culture. In 1903–6 she was taken to London to complete her schooling, and became convinced—as did other writers both in New Zealand and Australia at the turn of the century—that the only avenue to artistic success lay through escape to Europe. Accordingly, after a short career of miscellaneous local publication, Kathleen Beauchamp migrated. In 1918, she married John Middleton Murry and in 1923, died of tuberculosis. Her stories are especially memorable for their intimate approach to the world of childhood. It is the late Victorian world of the 1890s, centered in Wellington with its parties, picnics, and trips across Cook Strait on the ferry, that such stories as "At the Bay," "The Garden Party," and "The Voyage" recall. In 1921, making plans for "my new book" which remained unfinished, she outlined a table of contents and indicated settings for nine stories; three of these were to take place in London and six in New Zealand, which was still her primary source and came more and more to be her lost Arcadia.

Her story materials, as Professor Ian Gordon reminds us, were "in the central tradition of the English novel, the affairs of everyday heightened by sensitivity and good writing."[2] If a woman (in her fiction) is not alone in the world, she is likely to be joined to a man, husband or otherwise, by emotional ties that are fragile. Inevitably, where children are concerned (and she shows us how much more awareness they often have than we are disposed to imagine), they are affected; and in their relations with one another, as well as with adults, there lies a special realm of which Katherine Mansfield easily became the queen. Her very careful techniques of construction, allowing for quick and apparently effortless shifts in point of view but controlling rigidly the "sense of always being inside the character,"[3] are matched with a natural but (partly because natural, perhaps) lyrical use of language. She "draws on the stratagems of poetry, notably an unobtrusive—but powerful—use of symbolism."[4] This did not happen immediately; her first book appeared in 1911, but it was not until the story "Prelude" (1916, published later in the *Bliss* volume, 1920) that her final mode of presentation was achieved. Her own comments on various stories reveal how much of herself she spent on her work:

"Prelude"—I try to make family life so gorgeous—not hatred and cold linoleum—but warmth and hydrangeas.

"The Canary"—I have just finished a story with a canary for the hero, and almost feel I have lived in a cage and picked a piece of chickweed myself.

"The Voyage"—One day I must write about Grandma at length, especially of her beauty in her bath—when she was about sixty. I remember now how lovely she seemed to me. And her fine linen, her scent. I have never *really* described her yet. Patience! the time will come.

"The Garden-Party"—I am sitting in my room thinking of Mother: I want to cry. But my thoughts are beautiful and full of gaiety. I think of *our* house, *our* garden, us children—the lawn, the gate, and Mother coming in. "Children! Children!"[5]

Apart from stories such as these, which are at the core of her best achievements, New Zealand gave her—through the "back-blocks"—three tales of violence, "The Woman at the Store," "Ole Underwood," and "Millie." Of these, Antony Alpers says,

Superficially the three New Zealand tales are murder stories, with the deaths occurring outside the actual narrative. More essentially they are penetrating studies in the psychology of what isolation in a raw, unbroken country can do to human beings.

They do, however, "lack facility of dialogue."[6] It has been remarked also of the earliest stories (*In a German Pension*, 1911) that "Bavarian" as they purport to have been, they were "clearly an early attempt to handle the characters and scenes of 'Prelude' and other New Zealand stories." For example,

The picture of Binzer peering with disgust into a "gully," filled with empty tins and fennel, and, as a result, composing "a letter to the paper," is one that fits with ease into the New Zealand landscape, though scarcely into the Bavarian.[7]

If expatriation was a tragic experience for Katherine Mansfield, contributing strongly to her illness and early death, quite the opposite should be said of Jane Mander, a woman eleven years older who left New Zealand at about the same time—not for London, but for New York, where in 1912 she entered Columbia University as one of the first students in the newly opened School of Journalism. She had already written one novel, "turned down with admirable promptitude by four [London] publishers," she later stated with the verbal incisiveness that grew sharper with age and illness. She was already thirty-five (the age at which Katherine Mansfield died), but did exceptionally well in her academic work as well as in the employ of the Red Cross during World War I. Meanwhile, in 1914–16 she had written *The Story of a New Zealand River,* the title a conscious parallel to that of *The Story of an African Farm* (1883) by Olive Schreiner, whose work she greatly admired. She would have been glad to be considered the Olive Schreiner of New Zealand—as indeed she might have been if public acceptance there had not been so hostile.

In Europe from 1923 into the early Depression years, Jane Mander wrote and published in New York and London all six of her novels: *The Story of a New Zealand River* (1920), *The Passionate Puritan* (1921), *The Strange Attraction* (1922), *Allen Adair* (1925), *The Besieging City* (1926), and *Pins and Pinnacles* (1928). By this time she was over fifty; her aged father (to whom she was always much devoted) in New Zealand needed care, and she was no longer in robust health herself. She returned to New Zealand late in 1932, took up domestic duties, and though she wrote some newspaper articles and reviews, her career was virtually finished for the remaining years before her death in 1949.

The Story of a New Zealand River (not unlike Olive Schreiner's story) is much concerned with feminism, presented through the chief character, Alice Roland. Alice makes the transition from Victorian primness into a liberal outlook after moving to a timber-milling community on a northern river, actually the Otamatea, where the author's father owned kauri timber mills. About Jane Mander's orchestration of the complexities in such a situation, Dorothea Turner has written:

The setting of *The River* and the author's inside knowledge of bush-felling give it standing as a documentary, and her promotion of Alice and of the various emancipations she stands for suggests that sociological fervor was one of the spurs that drove her through the writing. Her beliefs, motives, and affections, however, combine in the creation of characters who transcend the

immediate limits of time and region. The novel's stature and its permanent
claim lie in the viability of Alice and Tom Roland, and to a lesser extent in
Asia.[8]

Allen Adair, the book next in quality to her first, is set in the gum
fields of the North Island (containing extensive deposits of resin from
kauri trees), also used as a locale by William Satchell. The central
figure is a young businessman who, longing to strike out on his own,
becomes a successful storekeeper and trader in the gum-fields country. He marries an Auckland girl, feeling himself that the city "was
all very well" for short periods but useful chiefly because "it gave him
the sense of contrast and glorified the country in comparison."[9] The
marriage erodes, and quickly; Allen "could never understand that
women loved a row, loved argument, loved to be unhappy."[10] He also
fails to see that his wife Marion wants to respond but doesn't know
how. A subplot provides Allen some relief through the friendship of
a solitary gum digger, Dick Rossiter, until Dick's self-assumed guilt
in a murder case is cleared up by a deathbed confession—something
of an old-style deus ex machina. Rossiter's return to England is part
of the reason Allen consents to return to Auckland—anticlimax of a
sort, but realism as well, seeing that the father's death has brought
Allen a small fortune.

One more of Jane Mander's novels, *The Besieging City* (1926) will
be discussed here. After it has been summarized, it will be compared
with a novel appearing thirty-seven years later as an exercise in observing differences between early and near-contemporary fiction in our
century: both novels are about New York City, and both narrate the
experiences of a single woman from New Zealand in seeking work
and adjusting to life in the metropolis. *The Besieging City,* which as
the title suggests presents city life as multifarious and challenging, is
a fictionalized account of Miss Mander's New York years. Christine
(Chris) Mayne, English born but reared in Australia, has an eye for
natural beauty as well as a knack for making friends, some of whose
roles are important enough to extend beyond the city's boundaries.
She works for the Red Cross during the war at financial sacrifice, but
manages at the same time to break into the literary world with articles in a newly founded *Weekly Critic* and the publication of a novel.
Bustling with change, the city both undergoes the scourge of influ-
enza and celebrates the armistice and the end of the war. Chris is a
liberated woman with an independently honest approach to living,
including romance; in love with a successful architect, she declines

marriage rather than relinquish her independence and solitude. Lavish parties, famous restaurants, beautiful people in beautiful clothes contrast with the personal problems and emotional strain that are the undercurrent of big-city life. The following short paragraph introduces a description of New York's response to the first (unofficial) report of an armistice and end of World War I:

At any moment New York is a mental powder magazine that a spark of drama may blow up. It is the home of spontaneous combustion. Somewhere above the city there hovers a puckish spirit with the secret of a magic gas that in one moment may bring inflammation of the brain upon the town from the man on the fifty-seventh story of the Woolworth tower to the remotest engineer in a sub-sub-basement fifty feet below the pavement. No way else may one explain the New York of that Thursday afternoon.[11]

Shirley Maddock's *With Gently Smiling Jaws* (1963) is a simple tale of futile struggles in a tiny pocket of New York filled with the little people, the poor. Catherine Willis—interested in writing and acting, eager to break into television, determined to be independent and to diverge from the Willis family norm of settling for a husband and children—moves into a tiny apartment between a funeral parlor and a dry-cleaning shop. She makes friends easily in the multinational neighborhood; though people have difficulty in placing New Zealand, they do recognize her English background. She finds a job with Telepress, a television advertising venture being floated by an unscrupulous operator, Mr. Timperly, who somehow manages to spend only other people's money—even for the innumerable cups of tea he orders delivered. Her young man, Andrew, has a good position with the UN and would like to get married, but not until Telepress collapses and Catherine has had time to think things over in a short summer job in a Maine coastal resort, does she decide to accept him. Following is a brief slice of the New York City scene which Catherine knew:

It looked as though the street had been up for hours, for Saturday though not for work. Shouting children were playing hopscotch in front of the condemned block of buildings, housewives stood talking, their baskets over their arms, and Catherine had a curious feeling as she made her way towards the butcher's that she was invisible, that everyone was minding their own business and no one was the least concerned with hers. "Well, you ought to be pleased," she told herself as she stowed a small steak and a parcel of lamb chops in her bag. "For years you've complained about the Willises minding your affairs, and now nobody does, so you should enjoy it."[12]

Mander, it is already evident, deals with city life on a broad scale, introducing important events to which her heroine responds. Her position with the Red Cross is one of significance and responsibility. New York undergoes an epidemic as well as orgies of drinking, blending of sexes, and splashy new building programs. Coué-ism (autosuggestion for self-improvement, a French import) competes with the Peace Conference of Versailles. The heroine's social circle is made up of kind, intelligent, sensitive people—the sort, she feels, that the city gradually makes into New Yorkers. Two of her friends commit suicide, suggesting the tragic side of life that may overwhelm women with emotional problems. But somewhat masculine in her outlook perhaps, she welcomes the challenge of things. Maddock's account, on the other hand, is restricted almost entirely to personal problems with a limited view of "inside" business practices, the "gently smiling jaws" that come close to thuggery at times. By comparison, the life of the city is not broadly viewed or much developed. Is Catherine glad to leave New York? No, but she likes Maine too. New York is at least not put down, and presumably the couple will be returning to Andrew's UN job and domestic security. There is pathos in the book, at times, but hardly tragedy, together with a great deal of natural friendliness that would suggest a link with Mander. Catherine is considerably more of an extrovert than Chris and, in the end, more conventional; after her brief fling, with a fairly easy resolution of conflicts, she gives every indication of merging quietly into the social scene she has served as witness to. Back down under, in New Zealand, the Willises may breathe easily again. Chris, in what is a much larger, denser book, shows depth in numerous ways. At the end, though reluctant to leave her adopted city, she is bound overseas, ready for whatever else is new.

In the same decade with Jane Mander appeared Jean Devanny, who created a storm of public protest by describing in *The Butcher Shop* (1926) brutality and violence on a sheep station. She wrote no more New Zealand novels and soon left for Australia, where she continued publishing during the 1930s and 1940s.

Third among a trio of women expatriates was Robin Hyde (1906–1939) for whose problems the gesture of the ritual trip to London was not the solution. Born in South Africa as Iris G. Wilkinson, she was brought to Wellington, New Zealand, where she grew up. She worked on various newspapers for a period of ten years, chiefly as a woman's page editor, becoming progressively more dissatisfied and finally deciding to migrate. In 1938 she left for England via China (about which she wrote *Dragon Rampant,* published in 1939) and not long after her arrival died a suicide at age thirty-three. With the exception of her book on China, there is thus no part of her work not immediately the product of her New Zealand years. She was affected by cultural colonialism, however, equally as much as Katherine Mansfield and Jane Mander had been before her and like them felt forced to choose exile as her gesture of rebellion.

Critics agree that her first and last novels—*Passport to Hell* (1935) and *The Godwits Fly* (1939), both with titles symbolic of departure, of migration—are her best and that the three middle ones—*Check to Your King* (1936), *Wednesday's Children* (1937), and *Nor the Years Condemn* (1938)—are considerably below her best standards. *Passport to Hell* has as its central figure an outcast named Starkie—a man with, of all things, North American Indian blood in Maoriland. Of this novel, J. C. Reid has written:

Based upon the true story of Douglas Stark, an underprivileged youthful criminal who became a war hero of a kind, this *tour de force* vividly recreates the mood of soldiering and the character of battle. But its anger is directed not so much against war as against social injustice. And Starkie, son of a Red Indian father and Spanish mother, can hardly be taken as a typical Kiwi.[13]

It should be added that it is one of a very small number of war novels written by women, in New Zealand or elsewhere. *Check to Your King* is the fictionalized biography of an eccentric Frenchman, the Baron Charles de Thierry, who in the late 1830s set himself up as "Sovereign Chief of New Zealand," claiming kingship over a territory of some forty thousand acres at Hokianga (North Island) which he intended to colonize. *Wednesday's Children* is a fantasy built around lottery winners, and *Nor the Years Condemn* is a sequel to *Passport to Hell,* but lacks the force of its original. *The Godwits Fly* deals with the Hannay family, centering on Eliza Hannay, the author's alter ego. The godwits—marsh birds that leave the northern tip of New Zealand for Siberia at the end of summer—seem symbolic of Eliza's friends fortunate enough to be off to England. Gloria Rawlinson, who has compared an earlier version of the novel with the one finally published, relates how Robin Hyde despairingly referred to the first version as "that pudding" and only after trial and error, and a hard decision to abandon a slow-moving, adult-centered, reminiscential

manner of presentation, was able to produce the "brilliantly evocative
style of *The Godwits Fly* as we know it."[14] The following passage,
from a chapter about Eliza's stay in the hospital after breaking a leg,
affords a glimpse into the internal and external worlds the heroine
alternates between:

> On the balcony she began writing a novel, an overgrown fairytale about
> a little boy who fell off the earth and went wandering through space. She
> could see thickets and campfires for him, but the plot tailed off, and writing
> against the iron cradle made her tired. Mostly she lay quiet, or clicked to-
> gether the big wooden knitting needles Carly had brought her, with mauve-
> pearl wool to make a wrap. The wrap never got done. . . . Days were much
> better than the nights, when the red light pricked through the windows,
> and always somebody came moaning or retching out from the anaesthetics,
> and it was impossible to get morphine, she had had far too much, and was
> better now. Biddy Kissin lay a white restless mountain in her bed, a tap
> dripped, a little piercing pinprick that went cleanly into the brain. She had
> dreams in which she was always running, taking high fences and rocks with
> great, easy leaps, Jack-the-Ripper leaps, which yet left a dream-feeling of
> dreadful effort. Then terror came in. Lions and tigers were after her, and she
> had to stop and persuade them, with long, plausible arguments, not to tear
> her to pieces. Sometimes she simply hid from them, once or twice she
> triumphed over them and they let her ride on their backs, but the feeling
> of effort and fear was never gone.[15]

The novels of James Courage (1905–1963), most of them set in
Canterbury (South Island), are consistently rather gray performances,
rendered so by the author's memories of his New Zealand years (he
left as a young man, remaining in England after graduating from
Oxford). Generalizing about Courage's achievement, R. A. Copland
writes:

> There is a pervading tone of seriousness if not of sadness deriving from a
> sombre acceptance of hereditary influences upon personality. Comedy breaks
> out on the edges of the novels though cheerfulness never breaks in. The set-
> ting is Canterbury rather than simply the back-country, for in Canterbury
> there linger most deeply those memories of England which Courage found
> in himself and out of season chose to record, borrowing overseas manners to
> record his personal truths.[16]

The Fifth Child (1948) and *Desire without Content* (1950) are set in suburban Christchurch in the 1940s; then *Fires in the Distance* (1952)

moves both back in time to the early 1920s and into the Canterbury backcountry for its record of unhappy family affairs. In *The Young Have Secrets* (1954), the setting is a seaside town, the time 1914, and the plot an emotional tangle between Walter, a young boy, and the daughters of a schoolmaster. M. H. Holcroft, who analyzes this novel at some length, feels that Walter's desires—and intentions—to kill his tormentor Mrs. Nelson are to be taken seriously: "There's nothing puny or half-hearted in the boy's longing for violence and vengeance." Moreover,

We're inclined to forget, as we grow older, how much naked and uncontrollable anger can set young nerves quivering, and how easy it is for strong feelings (whatever their source may be) to flare into violence. . . . We have seen it happen in recent years in cases which have ended in murder, shocking the nation and winning us a little notoriety overseas.[17]

In *The Call Home* (1956), an expatriate returns to New Zealand. Courage's two final novels, published in 1959 and 1961, are not set in New Zealand. Not very sympathetically, H. Winston Rhodes sums up the content of Courage's New Zealand novels as follows:

In his five New Zealand novels a neurotic mother, disappointed and bored with a too protective attitude to a son, a father coarsened by "colonial" farming, virile but frustrated, a sweet and understanding grandmother, a masculine girl, a feminine boy, a male given to bouts of drunkenness, a wife repelled by masculine sexuality, a precocious child, are the familiar ingredients of a plot which has clearly been contrived in order to provide a form of case-book entertainment. However deeply the writer may have felt involved in the situations described, he has remained not only detached but also withdrawn, so withdrawn that the reader experiences discomfort from a technical control that leaves him uncertain whether he is intended to accept mawkishness, sexual symbolism and artifice with wry amusement or sympathetic intelligence.[18]

Perhaps before Courage is judged finally, his work will need to be considered in the light of what the 1960s and 1970s produced, with the question asked, were his novels idiosyncratic, or did they anticipate the use of such "controversial" subjects by writers already beginning to loom over the horizon?

Finally, among expatriate writers, there is the work of Dan Davin, who like Courage left his ancestral home in the southern-most part of the South Island to attend Oxford before World War II (in which he served) and afterwards remained in England for a career in publishing. Since he is still active, and since all of his books were published after 1945, he is discussed in a later chapter; but we mention him here as the expatriate showing the least "dislocation syndrome" of any among those discussed. Personal temperament no doubt enters in, but it is probably also true that expatriation having now become largely a matter of choice rather than imagined compulsion, residence abroad for the writer is nothing that very much worries either the writer or the audience.

Chapter Four
Home Front

Our literature cannot possibly be called introspective, and because of this, I venture to suggest that we are not an introspective people, nor have we imaginative insight. Imagination, of a kind, yes. Heroes and villains in sharp juxtaposition, involved plots and fantastic theories abound, but of real characters in whom we can believe there are none.

—Elizabeth M. Smith, 1939

During the depression years, New Zealand writers found their proper subjects and themselves as well. Third-generation New Zealanders, they were not yet free from inherited conflicts. Yet they were facing directly for the first time the challenge of their own society and environment and they saw their task, as, in Fairburn's words, that of being "willing to partake, internally as well as externally, of the anarchy of life in a new place and, by creative energy, to give life form and consciousness." Where before there had been scattered, isolated achievement, there was now a substantial corpus of work that could properly be called a literature. There was also an increasing audience for it as readers found in the writings of their fellow-countrymen not only their own feelings and aspirations given significant form, but assurance of further growth.

—J. C. Reid, 1968

Fiction in all countries reveals a steadily continuing presence of writers whose chief purpose is to tell a good story, one that will entertain its audience but that makes no claim to profundity: social criticism and/or psychological analysis such writers leave to others. Literary history commonly gives such writers little or no mention; yet they have claims that should not be completely ignored. Their light (sometimes humorous) fiction offers reading for pleasure or for escape of the kind many people need and would not receive from "problem" novels; and not infrequently their sales are such as to help publishers keep publishing, thus making possible the appearance of more pretentious books that possibly otherwise could never appear. For the best of this kind there is no need for apology.

Entertainers

The story of Frank S. Anthony (1891–1925) is one of a remarkable blend of courage and pathos, tinged—years after his death—with irony at posthumous success. Brought up in Taranaki (North Island), Anthony went to sea in the early 1900s as a deckhand; then when war broke out in 1914, he left his ship in San Francisco to make his way immediately to England and enter the navy. Severely injured, he was invalided home to New Zealand. Returning to Taranaki, he bought and developed an eighty-acre tract into a dairy farm on which he lived alone, working during the day and writing at night. In the early 1920s, he sold the farm and went to London, where his rural-life stories began to sell. But the English climate proved less hospitable than the publishing world; in mid-January of 1925, he died there.

Anthony's Taranaki novel, *Follow the Call,* appeared under a New Zealand imprint in 1936. A collection of stories in 1938 "had a restricted sale and merited a much wider audience than it achieved," says a prefatory note to *Me and Gus* (1951), the book that at long last found the "wider audience" twenty-six years after the author's death. Anthony's sketches were edited and, at times, enlarged by Francis Jackson.

The "me" of *Me and Gus* is Mark Hendrick; Gus Tomlins is the neighbor who, although willing to tackle anything that comes along, never manages to do anything right—as, for example, when having bought a bull (left overnight at Mark's place), he comes to collect the animal.

The bull was still too wild to lead, and Gus seemed to fancy that was my fault too. He said it seemed queer to him the way the bull played up if anyone went near him, almost as if he had been knocked about.

I didn't like the suspicious way Gus looked at me when he said that. I asked him if he thought I'd spent the night prodding the thing with a stick, and he said: "Oh, no, no. Only he shouldn't be as wild as that!" Gus had seen hundreds of bulls ringed and tied up to a post for the night and they all tamed down by morning.

We tied a post on to the end of the chain in the finish and then let the bull out, and he dragged that post over to Gus's place by his nose. He made pretty good time, too, and if he hadn't got the post jammed across Gus's calf-paddock gate, I doubt whether we would have caught him again. Gus tied him up to the fence and expressed himself as satisfied.

"Mark," he said. "It's a good job it was me who bought this bull; you would never have handled him."

Not a word of credit for me or Ned. A man ought to cut out trying to help Gus Tomlins.[1]

Follow the Call is a plain man's love story, similarly lighthearted and episodic, which turns out happily.

Two women novelists, Rosemary Rees and Mary Scott, have provided a long list of generally romantic light fiction in which the New Zealand background is exploited. Of Rees's books, Elizabeth M. Smith had to say in 1939:

She makes plentiful use of country race-meetings, sheepshearing scenes, and the morning-teas and bridge-parties of would-be smart people in small country towns, but her characters, especially the hero and heroine, very rarely ring true. They are not New Zealanders. She has made use of New Zealand as Miss Sheila Macdonald has of South Africa. Having hit upon some external characteristics and been successful with a first book, both are content to repeat the same setting and almost the same plot as many times as their publisher will let them.[2]

Mary Scott's formula, as described by Joan Stevens, is not so very dissimilar: she stylizes the city-bred misfit who must be made over from scratch, if he (or she) is to succeed in the country. Still, her novels "for all their shallow portraiture, have gaiety and life, with flashes of perception, and with enough information about country goings-on to build up some picture of what the North Island backblocks are like."[3]

Better known than any of the previous three is Ngaio (a native botanical first name) Marsh, who had a very distinguished double career as a producer of Shakespeare (both in Britain and in New Zealand) and a writer of mystery novels. Her autobiography, *Black Beach and Honeydew* (1966) serves to expand our knowledge of her career in addition to revealing other aspects, especially those associated with theater. It also develops at length a picture of South Island (Christchurch) gentility not so very different from that which Katherine Mansfield knew at Wellington. Miss Marsh was born and educated at Christchurch, where she studied dramatic art and later became an actress and producer. During World War I, she served with the Red Cross transport services (recalling Jane Mander in New York), and afterwards continued her work in the theater. In all her stories, says Joan Stevens,

. . . the backgrounds are brilliantly drawn, while the puzzles posed by her
plots rise convincingly out of them. So it is with the New Zealand
trio. . . . The English theatrical scene however seems to provide Ngaio
Marsh with more of those eccentric or outrageous characters whose presence
makes her yarns so sparkling.[4]

The New Zealand setting of *Colour Scheme* (1943) is a North Island
spa much like Rotorua. Maoris (including an aged leader) figure in
the story through the machinations of a businessman who is secretly
removing native treasures from *tapu* ground on Rangi Peak. Not altogether undeservedly, he meets his end by being thrown into a pool
of boiling mud. By the Maoris? No, but it takes a plot involving
wartime espionage to reveal who the murderer was. This novel uses
the theater, as well, through the visit to the area of an eminent
Shakespearian actor, Geoffrey Gaunt, one of whose staff men has
some interesting things to say about actors in general:

"The thing about actors, for instance, that makes them different from
ordinary people, is that they are technicians of emotion. They are trained
not to suppress but to flourish their feelings. If an actor is angry, he says to
himself, and to every one else, 'My God, I am angry. This is what I'm like
when I'm angry. This is how I do it.' It doesn't mean he's angrier or less
angry than you or I, who bite our lips and feel sick and six hours later think
up all the things we might have said. He says them. If he likes someone, he lets them know it with soft music and purring chest notes. If he's
upset he puts tears in his voice. Underneath he's as nice a fellow as the next
man. He just does things more thoroughly."[5]

Died in the Wool (1945) is set on a sheep station, Mount Moon, where
the body of the owner's wife, Flossie Rubrick, is found neatly se-
creted in a bale of wool. Again, there is background from World War
II, here related to a military invention.

Bracketing the name of Ngaio Marsh with several other new writers (as of 1939—her career began in the mid-1930s), Elizabeth M.
Smith remarks that there was "a facility in the writing which leads
one to hope for better things from them."[6] A canny estimate, as
things turned out, for one of the group. By 1946, J. C. Reid was
able to say that she showed "intelligence and craftsmanship of a high
order which make her work outstanding in its sphere."[7]

Among other writers of suspense and crime fiction using the New
Zealand setting, critical opinion places Dorothy Eden (whose writing

career paralleled that of Ngaio Marsh both in chronology and in volume) as next in rank.

Chroniclers

The contemporaries of Katherine Mansfield and Jane Mander included two other women—not expatriates—whose work served the purpose of capturing the atmosphere of twentieth-century New Zealand in a lower key. The first, Blanche E. Baughan, in *Brown Bread from a Colonial Oven* (1912), produced a series of rural sketches which show, in McCormick's words, "evidence of a mind unusually aware of significant themes and related technical problems,"[8] as well as ability to use colloquial language with skill and to portray the Maori sympathetically. A more recent critic, P. C. M. Alcock, calls the author "a true colonial voice," observing that she

. . . reveals not only a rather high descriptive skill but an ear for dialogue and idiom, an adequate narrative sense for pace and climax, and a capacity for partaking others' lives which goes hand in hand with a simplicity of sentiment evidencing humility, humanity and integrity rather than mere simpleness or bathos.[9]

Some time later, Alice F. Webb in *Miss Peter's Special* (1926), under "conditions for the expression of a slender though admirable talent," wrote short pieces recording "the scenes, manners, social recreations, personalities of a peaceful community, described with humour but without sentimentality."[10]

Maori fiction continued to be written (still by Pakehas, of course), not so convincingly as in Satchell's *The Greenstone Door,* but at least with a growing regard to historical authenticity. Frank Acheson's *Plume of the Arawas* (1930) is blood-drenched enough, but not as between Maori and Pakeha, since it is set in pre-European times. The problem of racial mixture is explored again (as it had been for some decades) in F. Eric Baume's *Half-Caste* (1933): Ngaire, a half-caste girl, has as many troubles as some of her predecessors (who, however, were often princesses, as she is not), but she does manage at last to make a happy marriage to a Scot. Neither of these novels manages to bring the Maori theme much closer to maturity of approach.

Nelle M. Scanlan's *Pencarrow* (1932) is the first in a series of four about the Pencarrow family, beginning in the 1880s with Matthew Pencarrow, a farmer in the Hutt Valley near Wellington. The novel came into being as the result of a discussion between the author and her London publisher, Robert Hale, who had already brought out two of her novels, set in London. Why, he wanted to know, didn't she use New Zealand as a setting? She replied that New Zealanders weren't interested, which surprised and puzzled him enough to ask, nevertheless, that she do a New Zealand story for him, and *Pencarrow* was the result. Like Mazo de la Roche in Canada, developing her "Jalna" series at the same time, Miss Scanlan discovered she *could* create New Zealand characters to whom her readers would relate: Kelly Pencarrow, for instance, devoted to the land, and, by contrast, his sister Genevieve, a lawyer-intellectual. Her book, as Alan Mulgan puts it, "opened wider a door that was little more than a crack."[11] It contains a good deal that falls somewhere between sociology and editorial moralizing, as for example:

> The day of the Remittance Man is now over; the public school boy has come. Yet in some ways he was the prototype. But a changing world has almost erased his name, and the sins of the Remittance Man, who lived from cheque to cheque, waiting for the brief burst of glory and forgetfulness it brought, finds small place in the calendar of the pioneers of to-day. These mingle with New Zealand-born sons in the fulfilment of their common task. The public school boy of to-day is trained to work. The Remittance Man of last century was ill-equipped. He could not trade his Homer for a sack of flour.[12]

John Guthrie's *The Little Country* (1935) is somewhat of an anti-Pencarrow, a satirical approach to the "New Zealand tradition" in which the characters bear names like Sheepshed, Glanders, Watchitt, Boadicea Frippleton, and Mrs. Humphrey Spiral; one of the chief place-names is Cod's End. The people spend their time in elaborate social gestures, celebrating historical anniversaries, commemorating the Empire Builders, entertaining titled visitors from "home," and so on. At intervals (for example, in the opening section of Chapter 5), the author contributes his own comments on the littleness of nearly all the inhabitants of the Little Country—citing as an instance the endless (and pointless) municipal competition between Auckborne and Wellingford or between the North and South Islands, the latter sardonically qualified: "The rivalry between the two islands in late years, however, has been good-natured, and ill-feeling arises to-day only if the North Island gets more men in the All Black rugby football team than the south."[13]

Guthrie is by no means the earliest satirist of New Zealand society, but his book does mark the approximate beginning of a sustained barrage that still continues. Through the whole of the twentieth century up to the 1930s and well back into the nineteenth, it would not be unfair to say, a great many New Zealanders seem to have carefully preserved all the complacent stuffiness they inherited from their Victorian forebears (even as the westering pioneers carried puritanism from New England to the American Midwest), as well as inventing some of their own. This, after the freewheeling 1920s, was quite certainly destined to be attacked, with so little result, however, that the intellectuals' exasperation mounted all the higher. The bourgeoisie, accused of avarice, gluttony, and sloth, for the most part merely slothfully ignored their critics but nevertheless thought them motivated by pride, wrath, and envy, leaving lechery to be more or less evenly distributed between both parties to the quarrel. Guthrie, subsequently, published other novels—*Paradise Bay* (1952) and *The Seekers* (1952). Reviewing his entire output in 1954, Bill Pearson concluded: *"The Little Country* and *Paradise Bay* will always have a modest place in New Zealand Writing. The rest of Mr. Guthrie's work vanishes in the yearly output of English novels."[14]

Social Analysts

Satire brings us close to more serious fictional approaches to society, which, though they had not been entirely lacking in New Zealand writing, commenced about the time of economic depression in the 1930s to take firmer tone than previously. The youth-toward-maturity character study (not content to stop with childhood, as in Katherine Mansfield), which in the twentieth century has become a fertile theme, can be seen in New Zealand as early as the 1920s in the novels of Hector Bolitho, *Solemn Boy* (1927) and *Judith Silver* (1929), and a bit later in those of Alan Mulgan, *Spur of Morning* (1934), and C. R. Allen, *A Poor Scholar* (1936) and *The Hedge Sparrow* (1937).

In a different context, tending finally much further toward the political, is John A. Lee's *Children of the Poor* (1934), which "caused its author to be attacked with more violence and venom than any New Zealand novelist before or since has experienced."[15] The dedication reveals, graphically, both the content and tone of the book:

To daughters of the poor; to errant brats and gutter-snipes; to eaters of leftovers, the wearers of cast-offs.

To slaves of the wash-tub and scrub-brush, whose children, nevertheless, go
to hell.
To teachers who adopt, through compulsion or desire, the method of the
barrack square.
To juvenile culprits fleeing from the inescapable hand of the law, sometimes
called justice.
To that world of superior persons whose teeth have never been sharpened by
deprivation, whose sensibilities have never quivered from the shame of
their poverty.
In particular, to those whose birth—inexcusable audacity—may have of-
fended against Holy Law; whose life, against Man's . . .
THIS STORY OF THE GUTTER.
"A bastard shall not enter into the congregation of the Lord."
                                                                Old Testament
"Suffer little children, and forbid them not, to come unto me: for of such
is the kingdom of heaven."
                                                            New Testament[16]

Lee's autobiography, *Simple on a Soapbox* (1964), is dedicated to Up-
ton Sinclair, "who found me my first publisher." That in itself may
help identify Lee's brand of politics, which the title of another book,
Socialism in New Zealand (1938), makes perfectly clear. His most popular work of fiction, *Shining with the Shiner* (1944, reissued in a new
and expanded edition as *Shiner Slattery,* 1964) was written at the time
he was conducting *Lee's Weekly* and continuing generally as a none-
too-popular gadfly. *Shiner Slattery* is anecdotal fiction under a total of
eighteen sketch-titles such as "The Life, Times and Legend of the
Shiner," "Was Shakespeare a Hedge Cutter?" "At the Sign of the
Technicolor Liver," and "Luxury Is the Mother-in-Law of Invention."
Observing in his introduction that the Shiner "belongs to pioneer history, but the legend of the Shiner belongs still more,"[17] Lee accounts
for the presence of his rogue-hero by this logic: "Given wit and guile,
and a measure of good will amongst the hard workers, for all were
hard workers when they could find jobs, there was room for one
champion loafer, one who could as assiduously evade as others sought
steady employment."[18] There is not space here for the numerous il-
lustrations of the ingenuity through which this Irish jig-dancer lived
by his wits, but the remarkable time span of the book should be
noted: arriving from the Australian goldfields about 1870, Slattery
found a New Zealand population of a quarter of a million, the bulk
of whom had arrived during the previous decade (that of the New

Zealand gold rushes, especially to the South Island); and when he died at eighty-seven, in 1927, it was a million and a half.

Lee will undoubtedly retain a firm place in the hearts of many New Zealanders, especially for *Children of the Poor* but for some of his other works as well. Denis Glover, writing in 1951, recalled:

> When first published, during the depression, *Children of the Poor* awoke an immediate response in the minds and hearts of readers. All the parallels were there. It was realized that poverty was far-reaching in its effects, that the will to work was, in the absence of any work, no pointer to sturdy independence. And the story of his childhood, told by a boy whose sensitivity and personal bewilderment turned him into a creature of despair and then into a thief and outlaw, held its grim lesson as well as its poignancy.[19]

In summary of Lee's lively contribution to New Zealand fiction, K. O. Arvidson's comment on *Children of the Poor* will serve for Shiner Slattery as well:

> Notwithstanding its faults, its repetitions, its occasional gaucheness even, *Children of the Poor* is a triumphantly human novel. Its triumph is a stylistic one, and it is so precisely because its style is not a glass for looking through, but a function of Mr. Lee's personal vision itself, informing the novel in its every aspect. I doubt if we can afford to hold a book like this as merely a period piece.[20]

M. H. Holcroft, who has examined at length the varieties of childhood experience occurring in New Zealand fiction into the mid-1960s, sees three main tendencies taken by novelists and storywriters after Katherine Mansfield's work in the 1920s: the emphasis on the need to be respectable, the ordinariness of most New Zealand homes (especially as shown by the fiction of Davin), and a good deal of economic precariousness (explored by Lee and Ballantyne in the earlier years of the twentieth century and the Depression).

Margaret Escott, who published three novels in the 1930s—*Insolence of Office* (1934), *Awake at Noon* (1935) and *Show Down* (1936)—after which she wrote a great deal more but destroyed her manuscripts, was, like Lee, much interested in social justice. *Show Down*, recently reprinted (1973) in Auckland-Oxford's New Zealand Fiction series of revivals, "for directness and vitality, too, is not readily matched in our young literature,"[21] says Robert Goodman. The story is about dairy farming in the Waikato area (below Auckland) but

even more about the apparently ideal marriage of Anna Trove and
Dave Hawkes which gradually deteriorates through a web of errors.
This, properly enough, occupies most of the book, but occasionally
the wider world enters in, as in Dave's recollection of the earlier part
of the marriage:

> I've said we knew many things together, but in time we grew to know
> much more. We took the best of our own separate worlds and gave them to
> each other—not consciously, but just inevitably because we were so close to
> one another. Anna gave me things I'd always wanted and never had—the
> beauty and the smoothness and the courtesy of her life she gave me. I was
> hungry for those things and I took them eagerly. In return I woke in her
> the consciousness of the life outside her own, the poverty and the hardness
> and the bitter power that holds men down in the dirt and kicks them where
> they lie. I showed her some of the letters I got from Home and I told her
> what I knew of the War. She didn't say much, but I watched her come
> alive, I watched her grow as great in this new consciousness as she grew in
> her love.[22]

From Lee and Escott it is an easy transition to the work of Frank
Sargeson, who according to D'Arcy Cresswell was "the first wasp with
a new and menacing buzz" and who for more than forty years continued to excite and irritate. His view, as Bill Pearson says, is compas-
sionate but at the same time recognizes that humanity is perverse.[23]
He began with the brief narrative sketch, in *Conversation with My Uncle* (1936), and remained very strong at short fiction though publishing full-length novels as well: *I Saw in My Dream* (1949), *Memoirs of
a Peon* (1965), *The Hangover* (1967), and *Joy of the Worm* (1969).
Rhodes, remarking on Sargeson's attraction to the picaresque tradition, compares him with Dickens and Smollett and is likewise aware
of his very careful attention to the cadences and diction of everyday
speech:

> Because Sargeson was at first possessed with the idea of the importance of
> language through which his impressions of life must be communicated, he
> discovered that he was beginning to write in a manner completely different
> from any he had formerly achieved. He was beginning to create. He was
> finding a new voice, a voice which was at one and the same time individual
> and typical, which harmonized with the material which was becoming more
> and more part of his life.[24]

Rhodes's analysis is stated in terms of growth and emergence, neither one without struggle, which are at the core of everything Sargeson published and which, naturally enough, relate more closely to the young. But human effort is not as inexorable as the process in nature by which a root can penetrate and split a boulder; defeat and frustration await many of his characters at the hands of stern traditions. Sargeson remained the implacable opponent of overeasy optimism as well as puritanical repression, both endemic to the New Zealand national outlook. Heads-up realism, if anything, is what it takes to win, or to understand, which is one form of winning. The young narrator at the beginning of a novelette, "That Summer" (1946), has something of this viewpoint, as well as speaking the language Sargeson records with so much care and skill:

> It was a good farm job I had that winter, but I've always suffered from itchy feet so I never thought I'd stick it for long. All the same I stayed until the shearing, and I quit after we'd carted the wool out to the station, just a few bales at a time. It was just beginning December and I had a good lot of chips saved up, so I thought I'd have a spell in town which I hadn't had for a good long time, and maybe I'd strike a town job before my chips ran out.
> The old bloke I was working for tried hard to get me to stay but there was nothing doing. I liked him all right and the tucker was good, but him and his missis were always rowing, and there was just the three of us stuck away there with hardly any company to speak of.[25]

Other works by Sargeson will be discussed in a later chapter, but enough has been said here to emphasize Rhodes's observation that although the short works have meanings separate to themselves, there is a larger meaning "apparent only when the single stories are seen within the framework of the New Zealand setting, and the revelation of and commentary on New Zealand life are recognized as essential elements of the whole Sargeson world of imaginative realism."[26]

A writer who might well have risen quickly to share Sargeson's world of imaginative realism was John Mulgan (1911–1945), whose one novel, *Man Alone* (1939), was published in London just in time for most of the plates and stock to be bombed out of existence in the early days of World War II. Ten years later it was republished through the combined efforts of a New Zealand firm and the State Literary Fund. *Man Alone,* to which Mulgan had originally assigned the title "Talking of War," has as its hero "a nondescript twentieth-century Everyman, whose ordinariness is from the beginning insisted upon," as Paul Day reminds us.[27] Johnson, an English veteran of World War I, has come to New Zealand in 1919 to seek a new start in life. What he finds is "a quietness and sickness over everything"— hard to explain though not impossible to live with for a man of his temperament. He has jobs on several farms, affording Mulgan the opportunity of surveying New Zealand farm life in some depth. At length an employer's wife finds him more attractive than her husband, and during a confrontation the husband is accidentally killed by his own gun. Johnson flees and for many weeks lives in the bush, which seems to do its best to kill him but does not succeed. He leaves New Zealand undetected, having meanwhile experienced some urban violence as well (during unemployment riots in Auckland), and returns to Europe.

In the wider view, *Man Alone* was a preliminary sketch by a painter whose subject was man in society. Determined to write only of what he personally knew, Mulgan was obsessed by the search for ways of solving the problem which he saw as fundamental for mankind: the problem of establishing a just society in which the individual could grow in reasonably civilized peace. As Dan Davin has put it: "The unemployment riots . . . for an honest, ardent, generous mind . . . would never be over."[28]

As we shall see in later chapters, Mulgan's unease about New Zealand society—a young man's response to the events of the Depression of the 1930s—was to become, crescendo, a major concern of novelists after World War II, which Mulgan did not survive. It is this quality in *Man Alone* that makes it so clearly a landmark in New Zealand fiction.

Chapter Five
Racial Mixing Bowl

New Zealand, it is plain, has no future as a watered-down tasteless Britain of the South. It is as a genuinely Pacific society of mixed blood, mediating between east and west, that we may hope for its emergence in time to come with gifts of its own to offer the world. If we can free ourselves of some of the obsessive preoccupations and limitations of the present day by looking back to our origins and considering our place in the life of man—by taking a view of history that leads to freedom and not to servitude—we may come to understand our situation better and find what work for the future we can as a people most usefully undertake.

—*Landfall* (editorial), June 1953

"Well," said the young man, smiling. "We were the people before."
"I don't get you. You are trying to tell me you owned this place?"
"That's right. We owned all the land round this end of the river. Our tribe."
"That must have been a hell of a long time ago."
"Yes," agreed the stranger. "A long time." He was pleasantly spoken and patient. His round face, which I could imagine looking jolly, was very solemn just then.

—Maurice Shadbolt,
"The People Before," 1963

The years following World War II have been for New Zealand in many respects a moment of truth, a plunge into new domestic responsibilities as well as a time of international gains and losses. Among all the British "dominions," she would have been the most content to remain under the imperial umbrella; but as it soon became apparent, that shelter no longer existed. The Pacific, moreover, did not return to a recognizable resemblance to its former state; there were wars in China and Tibet, then in Korea, then in Vietnam, Laos, Cambodia. Long accustomed to being regarded as one of the "developing" nations, New Zealand found itself among a collection of elder states with responsibilities toward an increasingly sensitive, not to say explosive, Third World.

The earliest fiction about Maoris, we have already observed, set a pattern for either light romance or heavier "dying race" pathos well into the twentieth century. Bill Pearson's careful essay, "The Maori and Literature 1938–65," documents continuation of the old attitudes completely, both from novels and short stories. A bit later, the blood-and-thunder tradition of Maori fiction may be seen to survive in examples such as Barry Mitford's *Moana* (1975). Keeping this in mind we must not assume that there has been any sudden reversal that would have yielded consistently unbiased, well-informed treatment from all writers. Some of the newer fiction is good, some mediocre or hopelessly out of date. What we do encounter, however, is writing by Maoris themselves or, more accurately, by Polynesians, since Samoan New Zealanders are also commencing to write and publish.

Two novels published in the early 1960s, both in London, illustrate a lingering fidelity to the old image: Frances Keinzly's *Tangahano* (1960) and George Joseph's *When the Rainbow Is Pale* (1962), the second based on a fair amount of historical fact. Among the other Pakeha writers—still more numerous than the native ones, as they must continue to be for quite some time—we may distinguish a trio (Finlayson, Hilliard, Braithwaite) who approach the Maori with a degree of resolution evident from the number of titles published and a secondary group whose work, so far, has not proved so sustained. Roderick Finlayson, the eldest of the trio, published his first book of Maori stories, *Brown Man's Burden,* in 1938, following it with another collection, *Sweet Beulah Land,* in 1942. Since that time, two other books—*Tidal Creek* (1948) and *The Schooner Came to Atia* (1953)—have appeared. Finlayson (who has Maori ancestry) suggested in his first book that the Maoris, through their continuing identification with the soil and their birthplace, have been able to maintain a surprising hold, which nevertheless is precarious and is being gradually destroyed, partly through pressure from the whites, partly through conflicts of their own which have always been part of their culture. He writes, says Joan Stevens, "with a subtlety and understanding on the conflict between social values, on the simple verities, on the problems of those who live on the margins of society."[1] In *The Schooner Came to Atia,* the setting is not New Zealand but an imaginary island where a missionary, the Reverend Thomas Hartman, overcome by desire for a native girl Ima (his convert), becomes unbalanced and shoots her younger lover when he finds them together.

The Resident Agent conveniently finds the death accidental, and the Reverend Hartman and his wife soon leave for other territory. The white man's reputation has been upheld.

Noel Hilliard's novels and stories, taken together, give a more or less continuous picture of contemporary Maori culture. *Maori Girl* (1960) received mixed critical reaction because it was felt to be too much an indictment of Pakeha society, with the heroine, Netta Samuel, used mostly for that purpose. Pearson, however, observed that the book offered "the first serious examination of the Pakeha conscience in race relations in the city [where Netta is mistreated], and the opening chapters of Netta's life in the country are entirely new ground for a Pakeha writer" as well as "the first approach to common ground with Maori writers"—thus a landmark.[2] This book and *Power of Joy* (1965) and *Maori Woman* (1974) make up a trilogy. *Maori Woman* brings Netta Samuel back to the city again, where she takes up for a time with Jason Pine, a Maori newly out of jail, who proves unreliable, domineering, and at times violent. He has established also a liaison with a white girl, a friend of Netta's, but when he learns that Netta wants to leave him for a white man, violence erupts. One would judge that Hilliard is skeptical of most Maoris' chances at the good life if Netta's is a fair case. *A Night at Green River* (1969) takes a cross section of Maori life during a twenty-four-hour span, intended to summarize and typify it in contrast with Pakeha life. A collection of stories, *Send Somebody Nice,* appeared in 1976.

The Maori Wars of the 1860s, that hardy perennial topic of New Zealand novelists, was attempted again in the 1960s—almost as a centennial gesture, one is tempted to think, but with gratifying success—by Errol Brathwaite, also the author of novels related to World War II (*An Affair of Men,* 1961, and *Long Way Home,* 1964). The trilogy begins with *The Flying Fish* (1964), which made "a genuine imaginative penetration into material that usually stimulates our writers only to romantic rhetoric or fiendish bloodbaths," says Joan Stevens, emphasizing the mutation from previous tradition.[3] *The Needle's Eye* (1965) goes on into the deepening phases of the struggles, with *The Evil Day* (1967) chronicling the last organized resistance of the Maoris, the Hauhau guerrilla movement. In the final volume, after many isolated attacks on both sides, the use of hostages, rumor spreading, and other techniques including brutalities familiar enough to a twentieth-century audience, the stronghold of the Hauhau chief,

Titokowaru, is reached by Colonel Williams who expects a major engagement but finds the *pa* deserted except for a few stragglers, one of whom is seized and brought for questioning:

"If many wish to kill me," Williams said, "why do they let me take Te Ngutu-o-te-manu so easily? Why do they not fight?"
"Why should they fight for that which they do not value?"
"Not value Te Ngutu-o-te-manu? Titokowaru's stronghold?"
"It is no longer Titokowaru's stronghold," the old man said. "It was too far for the *Pakeha* to come to fight, so perhaps Titokowaru has gone to fight the *Pakeha*, because he was tired of waiting. He has gone."
"Where has he gone?" Williams asked.
"You are Ihu Kaka, the Parrot Beak," the prisoner replied. "Smell him out."
Williams felt a glow of admiration for the old warrior's show of spirit, but he kept his voice level and cold, and shrugged his shoulders.
"If you do not tell me," he said, "perhaps I shall hang you from the *niu*."
"So many chiefs have died the death that it is an honourable one, at your hands," the old man said evenly. "I am old, anyway."[4]

Phillip Wilson, in *Beneath the Thunder* (1963) and *The Outcasts* (1965), has explored marriages between Maori and Pakeha which end disastrously, leaving the younger Maoris, in particular, much embittered. Of *The Outcasts,* Pearson says: "The parts of this novel that are most convincing are the reactions of the Waikato landowners to their daughter's love for a Maori and her own motives for loving him, in rebellion against their narrow code."[5] Wilson has also explored the theme in short stories.

Quite a different atmosphere pervades the books of E. H. Audley, also evocative of Maori culture in the 1960s: *No Boots for Mr. Moehau* (1963) and *A New Gate for Mattie Dulevich* (1965). Both are easygoing stories in a familiar, even chatty sort of style. In the first, a land-sale controversy, ranging younger Maoris against older, is settled by bringing in a sympathetic public official. The second, also relating closely to land tenure, relates chiefly to the Duleviches, a Dalmatian farm family (now an elderly couple living by themselves), and old Amo, a guardian of Maori tribal lands. These people, living peacefully at Maratangi on a peninsula (Coromandel) at the top of the North Island, find themselves threatened by the grandiose plans of land speculators, "developers" who wish to turn the place into a pleasure resort. This assault the community, at length, repels.

A group of women writers in the same period have produced a series of works relating more or less directly to Maori life, beginning with Sylvia Ashton-Warner's *Spinster* (1958) and extending through Anne Holden's *Rata* (1965) and Jane Wordsworth's *Four Women* (1972) down to Patricia Grace's book of stories, *Waiaraki* (1975). *Spinster* deals with a teacher, Anna Vorontosov, who is in charge of young Maori children; it might be said without too much exaggeration that here at last is one Maori-Pakeha novel in which something constructive happens: Anna finds not only that she can relate to the children but that there are ways of teaching language to them that succeed where others fail. The book was a sensation at the time of its publication and still tends to eclipse the author's succeeding novels (which are discussed in a later chapter). *Rata* poses the age-old problem of the half-caste for eleven-year-old Rata Lovell, who in her orphaned loneliness seeks, and finds for a time, comfort among her Maori relatives; yet:

> From the very first day she'd had a sense of belonging, of kinship, but she knew now she had stayed there only as a visitor, although a welcome one. She realized at that moment that when you were a child, you could no more choose your home than you could choose what you were. A child had to live with the people who accepted her unquestioningly as their responsibility. You had to be what you were and make the best of it; running away was no good.[6]

Anne Holden's second novel, *The Empty Hills* (1967), also deals with the runaway urge, but is not about Maoris or half-castes. *Four Women* brings together, as neighbors and friends, two Maori women and two Pakehas, all married. Two love affairs involve a Pakeha coach at the school with a sixteen-year-old girl, Meri, at the same time his wife Sheila is being courted by a young Maori, Hone. This light but interesting novel affords a look at both cultures, showing strengths and weaknesses on both sides in a situation already far advanced into racial integration.

The early 1970s saw the emergence of fiction by three Maori and Samoan authors (at about the same time fiction by native New Guinea writers was appearing from Australian presses): Heretaunga Pat Baker, Witi Ihimaera, and Albert Wendt. This alphabetical arrangement also suits the historical chronology of their works. Baker's *Behind the Tattooed Face* (1975) portrays pre-European Maori life in the Bay of Plenty area in episodes of tribal warfare with a romance. In the final chapter, entitled "A Prophecy is Fulfilled," Cook's *Endeavour* anchors, and Tipu Tapeka, priest of the Raumoko tribe, tells his chief:

"Behind the tattooed face a stranger stands. He will inherit this world—he is without tattoo!"
"I cannot believe that day will ever come," said the young chief.
"It will," replied the priest.[7]

Cook's party lands shortly thereafter, and Chief Haukino Te Onewa, after a show of resistance (or what is mistaken for such), is shot dead. An author's note states that this novel "is planned as the first of several, drawing on the vast store of tribal tradition and legend."

Witi Ihimaera, after a volume of stories, *Pounamu, Pounamu* (1972), published two novels in rapid succession: *Tangi* (1973) and *Whanau* (1974). In the first, the death of Tama Mahana's father, Rongo Mahana, and the ceremonies *(tangi)* at his funeral combine in the author's words into "a poetic drama in prose, about a young man and his father . . . an account of death, but also an affirmation of life."[8] Realistically enough, emotion surges through the entire volume until, in a quiet moment just after the burial, the bond between father and son is recalled and reaffirmed in this passage (which constitutes all of Chapter 31):

If anything should happen to me, you must look after the family, Tama.
Yes, Dad.
You must come home. Your mother will need you. Your brother and sisters will need you too.
Dad, I will remember.
You are the eldest, Son. The eldest always looks after the younger ones of the family.
I understand, Dad.
I was taught that when I was a child. I teach you the same now. Never forget.
E pa, I will never forget.
Good boy, Son. You make me proud, ay?
I will be your son, e pa. I will make you proud, e pa. Haera ra, e pa. Haera ra.[9]

Whanau, in Maori, means "family" in the large, distributive sense that embraces a whole area. Set in Waituhi among the family of Kai, the book describes both present and past, introducing a large number of characters, young and old, whose problems and achievements are those of the community as well as their own. "Although Witi Ihimaera exalts and honours the dying whanau," says the reviewer in *Landfall*, ". . . he does not idealise the Maori. What he succeeds in doing is to present a fascinating and honest record of one day in the life of the whanau, threatened by disintegration from within and contamination from European values outside."[10]

In Ihimaera's *The New Net Goes Fishing* (1977), the stories turn toward the city to form the first (it is said) of a projected trilogy of urban Maori life.

Of Albert Wendt, the novelist-critic Bill Pearson writes: "Albert Wendt told me once that when he planned to return to Samoa a good many years ago some of his New Zealand friends predicted that he would 'vegetate in Eden.' His spirited novels prove how wrong they were."[11] Wendt's novel *Sons for the Return Home* (1973) and his stories *Flying-Fox in a Freedom Tree* (1974) are about family life too, but in a less integral fashion than in Ihimaera's books. Samoa is far enough removed so that a foreign residence of very long duration, commonly in New Zealand, amounts to exile. *Sons* is an unusual and haunting story, a simple yet amazingly powerful examination of love: social, Christian, physical, familial. The central figure, a conscientious, intelligent young Samoan boy, becomes deeply involved with a beautiful Papalagi (white) New Zealand girl, from a wealthy home. Family relationships as well as personal ones are sensitively dissected and described. Upon the return, this conversation takes place between father and son:

Chuckling unexpectedly, his father clapped his hands, and said in English: *"He was a weird bugger!"* For a moment he couldn't believe what he had heard. His father's very New Zealand remark seemed so incongruous, but it was—so he would later conclude—a most apt description of his grandfather. His father looked across at him and, smiling deeply, said in Samoan: "A strange fellow but you would have liked him and he would have loved you most out of all those he called 'his spineless descendants.' " His father paused. He felt uncomfortable under his scrutiny. "You look like him too. You've always reminded me of him. Even more so now that I've watched you trying to live in Samoa. But I've never told you that before, have I! Why?" He paused again. . . . "Because, I didn't really want you to turn out like him. True, I wanted you to be a doctor, a healer, like him. But I didn't want you to be like him as a man." He sighed and looked at the bare ground. "Aren't you going to ask me why? . . . I think you know already," he added slowly.

"Why?" he insisted. He had to hear it from his father.

Looking steadily at him, his father said: "Because he saw too clearly, too honestly. Do you know what I mean?"

"Yes," he admitted, and somehow the heat began to weigh lightly on his body. [12]

The impressive style and psychological perceptiveness of the novel are apparent as well in Wendt's book of stories, one of which was published as early as 1963 in a student yearbook. One reviewer could see links between the author and V. S. Naipaul, in that both "are writers of multi-cultural inheritances, and a needling sense of humour is at least a satisfactory anchor when conflicting cultural wave-patterns clash in a single mind."[13] A later book of stories, *Pouliuli* (1977), its title being the Samoan word for "darkness," takes Samoan society as its background. *Leaves of the Banyan Tree* (1979) uses a hard-driving native capitalist as protagonist—a tragic one, as it turns out. It is reassuring to be able to conclude this chapter, on the modern handling of a familiar theme, in the knowledge that possibly major talents have commenced to show us how those so long written about, given time, can in turn become themselves the writers.

Chapter Six
Fretful Sleepers

Here we are, in mid-ocean, adrift and alone, confused and talking loud, wondering where to go next. In the meantime perhaps, we hope to sleep it off.

—Bill Pearson, 1952

If New Zealand often seems a conservative arid country, and its politics, for one example, are frequently so, this relapse into convinced conformity, with its undercover of unsatisfied bitterness, may be part of the explanation. It may also help to explain the short creative lives of many who hope to become writers, and, more generally, what sometimes appears to be a frequent failure of promising men in their twenties to make a contribution equal to their talents during the next twenty years of their lives.

—Robert M. Chapman, 1953

Enough has already been said for the reader to be aware that New Zealand, for all its idyllic scenery and egalitarian society, is not a country in which mental health has kept pace with physical longevity. Where on earth, for all that, would we find a nation where it has? For one reason or another, however, it does seem that fiction in New Zealand, especially in the postwar years (but by no means exclusively so), reveals dislocations in the psyche on a scale that is inconsistent with a small but prosperous and still roomy country which seems to have rather minimal problems externally. In this chapter, whose title and first epigraph are taken from an essay originally notorious and now well on its way to being famous, we shall be reviewing some of the fictional versions (including one of the author's own) of what Pearson's hard-hitting prose had to say.

Owls, Penguins, States of Siege:
Janet Frame and Other Psychological Novelists

An expatriate, James Courage (1903–1963), is the earliest among a group approaching the troubled state of the New Zealand psyche after World War II. Born in North Canterbury, Courage lived and wrote in England during his adult life; but despite his long exile from

this area, it forms the setting for the bulk of his fiction. Character-
istically, he develops problem stories in which an apparently placid
surface is seen to mask a situation filled with psychological entangle-
ments. In *The Young Have Secrets* (1954), critics are agreed, this appears most notably. Walter, the ten-year-old central figure of the
story (which takes place about 1914), lives in a world of adults who
unburden themselves to him, thus making him feel pushed unnatu-
rally toward adulthood. Some relief from the tension is provided by
a friend, Jimmy (Nelson), who is "normal" enough not to care *what*
happens to adults; his somewhat blowsy mother and her Maori husband help keep the common touch. The "disturbed" adults include
a young architect in love with three sisters at once, a pompous old
schoolmaster who tries to make a little Eton of Walter's school, and
the master's class-conscious wife. *The Young Have Secrets* appeared after
two earlier books, *The Fifth Child* (1946) and *Fires in the Distance*
(1952). In *The Call Home* (1956) an expatriate New Zealander, Norman Grant, revisits North Canterbury after the loss of his wife but
finds most of his ties either broken or no longer meaningful. *A Way
of Love* (1959) undertakes the difficult theme of homosexuality, with
the result (as one critic, M. K. Joseph, sees it) that the novel is "a
quietly ruthless exposure of the pretensions of homosexuality, and a
sad book, despite its appearance of an urbane and sensual exterior."[1]
This novel, like his last one, *The Visit to Penmorten* (1960), is set in
England.

Courage's preoccupation with the abnormal may have helped pre-
pare for the acceptance of Janet Frame's fiction, which in its earlier
years was contemporaneous with Courage and, of course, Sargeson.
When Patricia Guest, *Landfall*'s reviewer of Miss Frame's first book,
The Lagoon and Other Stories (1951), came to sum up, she quoted a
sentence from the story "Jan Godfrey": "Everything is always a story
but the loveliest ones are those that get written and are not torn up
and are taken to a friend as payment for listening, for putting a wise
ear to the keyhole of my mind."

She went on to say that the effect of the book was to offer "an
opportunity to put a wise ear to the keyhole of a mind more sensitive
than one's own—an experience that induces respect and humility in
a reviewer."[2] The review ends with the qualified praise that this is
already a "considerable achievement" as well as "a promise of future
work of distinction, if she should discipline her style and exercise a
greater objectivity in the selection of her experience."[3] That is what

Janet Frame did not do, as luck would have it, and her next volume, the full novel *Owls Do Cry* (1957), received very high praise. It evokes the life of a dreary small town of the South Island, but compassionately and unsociologically. Speaking of the Withers family, central to the book, H. W. Rhodes says:

It is not merely that poverty and monotony, mental and bodily sickness, tragic death and slow decay, insensitive respectability, murder, and vagrancy crowd in upon them, but that of the two major characters with whom we sympathize one is "brought to the confusion of dream," and the other is "there and not there, journeying half-way which is all torment."[4]

Cherry Hankin, writing nearly two decades later, sees both situations and language in *Owls Do Cry* as interlocking in a "parable-like illustration of the imaginative individual [represented by the character Daphne] in an increasingly regimented society," with special emphasis on the surrender of meaningful human language to the voices of the automaton "media."[5]

The tormented, half-way journey was to be the pattern for most of what Janet Frame produced, which, in the twenty-year span following her first book, reached a total of more than a dozen volumes; she has continued to publish regularly. Many of the titles are indicative: *Faces in the Water* (1962, a girl's life in a mental home), *The Edge of the Alphabet* (1962, Toby Withers's and Zoe Bryce's failures to find an outlet abroad, but "One day we who live at the edge of the alphabet will find our speech"), *Scented Gardens for the Blind* (1953, mental illness again), *The Adaptable Man* (1965, in which criminality is the protagonist's mode of proving he belongs to his times), *A State of Siege* (1967, a retiring teacher flirts with the idea of independence on a Pacific island but is "besieged" by her own misgivings), *Intensive Care* (1970, a ravaged family's sufferings, counterpointed against a futurist fantasy world of eugenic ruthlessness). A comment by Margaret Dalziel on *Living in the Maniototo* (1979) observes that in linking war with the experience of growing up—"the loss of innocence and joy as we struggle with material necessity"—Janet Frame is using one of her primary motifs: Variations of this metaphor, along with the related ideas of invasion and siege, can be traced throughout her work, as an expression of a consistently dark view of men's lives.[6] And the ultimate delivery from suffering is never far out of this author's line of sight. "Curiously enough," says Patrick Evans,

Janet Frame gains stature as an author the further her work is removed from its regional provenance. Looking back, one could guess that without the tragic bereavements of her early years she might have become a minor novelist with a flair for satire but without a reputation overseas. As soon as death enters her vision, her art breaks the limitations of the provincial and begins to speak to all readers; her concern is not merely with what it means to be a New Zealander but with what it means to be a human being living in the twentieth century.[7]

Janet Frame's style is sui generis, not to be categorized as consistently either prose or poetry. In an early story entitled "The Triumph of Poetry" (reprinted in *The Reservoir and Other Stories,* 1963), both title and plot are ironical, or multidimensional, but they do suggest that her work has long been deeply involved with the metaphoric-poetic mode of expression, resulting not only in a volume of poems per se (*The Pocket Mirror,* 1967) but at length in whole chapters (as in *Daughter Buffalo,* 1973) cast in poetic form. She uses a prose-poetry that turns life upside down/inside out and bangs it against the stone-steel-glass-paper walls hemming it in to watch it peel off layers of itself. Hers is a deliberate effort to trespass conventionally accepted boundaries: poetry/prose, good/bad, success/failure, sanity/insanity, human/animal—the slash marks at length appear to dissolve, and the designations melt into one another, so much so, sometimes, that even her most inveterate readers and champions are uncertain of her meanings. Through most of her stories (not all, since she has lived abroad a good deal and as an "adaptable woman" used settings in England or New York), troubled humanity is looked at in New Zealand as if through the iridescent paua-shell eyes of a Maori carving, never reflecting quite the same from a slightly different angle.

Also deeply concerned with the disturbed and distraught in New Zealand experience is Maurice Gee, who with the publication of *Plumb* (1978) emerged as a novelist capable of handling the New Zealand historical scene together with personal predicaments and ideological conflicts over a wide range. The central figure, George Plumb, is a one-time Presbyterian minister turned rationalist and Unitarian as the result of libertarian tendencies which the backblocks of the South Island could not accept. Early in the narrative he reflects:

> What did I believe in those days? The doctrinal part is remote from me and when I try to bring it back seems so trivial I find it hard to believe two earnest and intelligent people exercised their minds on it ardently, as on a matter of life and death. But it was so.

Earnestness and intelligence lead Plumb and his beloved wife Edie to endure long deprivations and continuing ostracism, even a brief period of exile in California, through most of their lives including two wars and the Depression. Plumb judges himself sternly, both as Calvinist and freethinker, in ways that lend the story credence and compassion. We encounter through it an impressive sweep of colonial and postcolonial spiritual experience, not unrelated to political and social matters. The Plumbs' large family (twelve children) is seen by the father-narrator as objectively as humanly possible, with acknowledged and much-regretted blind spots. He is left, he tells us in the concluding chapter, unable to "re-enter the Light" but with at least "a knowledge and acceptance of my nature; a knowledge of the Cosmic order; and a fixed memory of my glimpse of God." There is, one might say, on the part of the author a firm knowledge and qualified acceptance of the strengths and weaknesses of his countrymen. *Plumb,* which won the 1979 New Zealand Book Award for fiction, is the first of a proposed trilogy. The second, *Meg* (1981), carries forward into more recent and more chaotic circumstances the family chronicle begun in *Plumb.*

Gee's earlier works include *The Big Season* (1962) in which the central figure Rob Andrews, football hero, befriends a criminal and two people with whom the man (a burglar) is associated, with the inevitable consequence that he is abruptly forced into defiance of social mores and finds himself an outcast; *A Special Flower* (1965), narrating the destruction of a middle-aged man by a late marriage with which he cannot cope; *In My Father's Den* (1972), the story of a murder committed in Wadesville, a mushroom industrial suburb of Auckland, in which the accused (falsely) is an English teacher whose student was the victim; and a volume of stories, *A Glorious Morning Comrade* (1975). *Games of Choice* (1976) describes the disintegration of a family.

Graham Billing is not quite such a connoisseur of loneliness as Janet Frame, but both in *Forbush and the Penguins* (1965) and in *The Slipway* (1974) that theme is important. In the first novel, the protagonist solves his problems for himself, alone in the Antarctic as a biological researcher. He has radio contact with Scott Base, writes and receives letters and supplies, but the penguins' survival gradually becomes an obsession as he notes the inroads on their numbers made by the skua-gulls, a sea leopard, and the elements. As the weather moderates, he begins to see life and death in calmer perspective; and when the rookery is finally silent, the penguins having departed, he can accept calmly the few moulting skuas still remaining. *The Slip-way*, set in a seaside town named Port Paradise, depicts in the char-acter Geoffrey Targett, owner of a declining coastal shipping line, a man who in middle age is descending into alcoholism. Commenting on this, the storywriter Maurice Duggan says:

> What energies of enterprise and organization he is able to command are devoted to an allegorical or at least symbolic solution [he will not scrap his last ship, but will give her to the Navy and Air Force for target practice]: the real and the illusory merge, separate and reform in his mind. He isn't mad, far from it: he isn't sober, by any means: the pressure derives from his difficulties in finding a solution dramatic enough to exhibit the true mag-nitude of his dilemma, of what in the corners of his soul it all means to him and of what, too, by meaning too much it has brought him to.[8]

Targett's behavior is death-wish, at least symbolically, but in *The Orderly* (1970), Gideon Cream, a part-Fijian orderly in a London hos-pital, is death-devoted. He sees it as supreme over life and (being impotent) as a replacement for sex. The book is divided into narrative sections, two of them—appropriately to the topic—interrupted by death. Here we would appear to have a kind of logical conclusion to a broad spectrum of psychological interests; or at least the wave mo-tions approach the point where ordinary sensibilities find them diffi-cult to perceive.

Suburbia and Sub-suburbia

New Zealand is not a country whose population lives predomi-nantly either on the land or in small towns; two-thirds of the people live in urban areas. As in many other places, however, the rural or small-town ethos remains strong, and while no bombshell quite like Sinclair Lewis's *Main Street* has rocked the two islands, Janet Frame's *Owls Do Cry* was a revelation that has had parallels. Ian Cross, in *The God Boy* (1957), uses as narrator an eleven-year-old boy, Jimmy Sul-livan, from a family living in a seaside town symbolically called Rag-gleton. Jimmy's parents are at each other's throats: the father drinks, the mother nags him, and finally the mother kills the father after a quarrel over his gift to Jimmy of a bicycle. Jimmy's "Why?" is well explored, E. H. McCormick believes:

The sense of injustice is the more acute because in a moment of revelation he has seen God in the class-room and counted himself among the chosen—a God boy. The treatment of this theme carries complete conviction. Jimmy's quarrel with God is the logical outcome of character and circumstance, and it is presented throughout strictly in terms of the child's perceptions. So Mr. Cross has explored what is, at least in this country, virgin territory, and with his small Promethean hero he has introduced to our literature a note of authentic tragedy.[9]

The Backward Sex (1960) and *After Anzac Day* (1961) also explore psychological themes in similar settings. In *After Anzac Day,* the central figure is a young girl, Jennie Page, mistreated but also befriended during World War II in the Wellington suburban area.

Bill Pearson's one novel (he has also published short stories), *Coal Flat* (1963), contains in fictional form some of the charges against New Zealand society that his essay "Fretful Sleepers" laid down ten years earlier: it is "an imaginative reconstruction of a whole community of a West Coast mining town," says Rhodes,

. . . revealing, in its parochialism, its resistance to ideas, its aesthetic and spiritual poverty, wider stretches of New Zealand life than might seem possible, and discovering aspects of character and attitude that are by no means contemptible. Pearson's achievement is not only that he has created a well-populated novelist's "world" in which the local characters are closely bound together by their prejudices and differences and involved in and excited by their small-town activities, but that he has created it without irony, accepted it in terms of itself and, without melodramatic distortion succeeded in touching life at so many points.[10]

The story is developed through the experiences of Paul Rogers, who returns to his West Coast home country as a teacher, falls in love, works hard with difficult pupils without reward or understanding, and is discouraged by the intensity and tenacity of a good many local mores, which he can do little or nothing to change.

A later writer, Joy Cowley, began her career with *Nest in a Falling Tree* (1967), in which one individual's situation is deeply probed by a "voice from the interior" method. Maura Prince, after her mother's death (in an old Wellington mansion), tries to find a new life with a young gardener-boarder, Red, as a kind of lover-son, but he leaves her. Finally and completely alone, she begins talking to her dead mother and reliving the past. Patrick Evans, who reviewed the book the year after its publication, pays tribute to the "intelligence and effectiveness" of her writing and compares her with Patrick White and Katherine Mansfield, also users of the spinster theme. In *Man of*

Straw (1970), a thirteen-year-old girl, Ros (Rosaling), finds herself
suddenly wrenched into a family crisis at a time when she is enjoying
life the most in a supposedly ideal family situation at Morris Bay. She
doesn't actually know what has been going on (that her father, a phi-
landerer, has been accused of sexual assault by one of her teenage
friends), but suddenly the whole atmosphere becomes so hostile and
negative that she runs away and hides in a cave by the sea, returns
upon falling ill, and becomes an even more tragic figure. Her state of
mind is described in these few sentences, which show us the devious
paths suburbia can sometimes take for itself:

Nothing made sense, but, then, it never had and never would. Every time
she made an attempt to define her parents' social position, she was con-
fronted by so many contradictions, such confusion, that she felt like a sparrow in a tornado. Later, when the dust had settled and she lay exhausted
amongst the feathers of her own questions, she would try to gather herself
together again by denying her mother's and father's existence. But that,
she'd discovered, was no solution either.[11]

Of Men and Angels (1972) is concerned with another domestic tangle
entailing suffering and sacrifice.

As comic relief to so generally agonizing a chronicle, perhaps at
this point the episodic fiction of Barry Crump should be mentioned.
Beginning with *A Good Keen Man* (1960) and *Hang On a Minute, Mate*
(1961), Crump—who once gave his address as "of no fixed abode"
and the list of his occupations as "farmworker, teamster, deer-
culler, timberworker, car salesman, tractor driver, rabbiter, crocodile
hunter, fisherman, beachcomber, compiler of fantasies"—has carried
the New Zealand flag for a type of rowdy, picaresque humor endemic
in a few writers from Maning's *Old New Zealand* in the 1860s to Anthony's *Me and Gus* in the late 1930s. Other books have continued to
chronicle what Joan Stevens describes as a "headlong hardcase Kiwi
career," and palpably on the side of the libertarians.

Several other novels using the small-town setting may be briefly
mentioned. David Ballantyne's *The Last Pioneer* (1963) brings an Englishman, Charlie Wyatt, to Mahuta in the hope of awakening the
place to self-improvement, but he fails and at length departs. At one
point in the book, he is given a brief anatomy of New Zealand small-
ness and dullness by a small-town editor. This asserts, in part:

I mean, why do you think we spend so much on boozing and betting?
. . . Because the safe life, you know, gives us the stitch. I mean, that long

white cloud you hear about at Royal Tour times can get to be *damned* grey. So we go on the booze. Or we go to the races. And to hell with the safe life! . . . I mean, suburbs are the same everywhere. And the pioneer is out of fashion. These days, when the immigrant steps down from his ship to Lambton Quay or Queen Street [Wellington or Auckland], he doesn't head for the bush, you know—he heads for Karori or Mission Bay.[12]

Earlier, Ballantyne (after 1955 an expatriate journalist in London) had surveyed a family situation in *The Cunninghams* (1948). Somewhat similarly to *The Last Pioneer,* Pat Booth's *Footsteps in the Sun* (1964) "lashes out in all directions at once" at small-town life. William Taylor's *Pieces in a Jigsaw* (1972) is set in Victoria, a suburb of Auckland, where Margaret Herbert, a teacher migrating from England, finds herself involved in more than she can handle as the result of a love affair with one of her students. Taylor's *The Persimmon Tree* (1972) examines family life in a rural community, especially a father-son relationship after the father has entered Russet Park, a home for the aged. Finally, in Margaret Sutherland's *The Fledgling* (1974), a solitary spinster-librarian in a "quiet" New Zealand town attempts to satisfy her maternal urges by stealing a baby. Summing up the whole direction taken by the novels described in this section, and others that might be cited, Rhodes writes:

> Novelists and short story writers have not been slow to detect features of a transplanted and distorted puritanism intertwined with middle class respectability, social conformity and an easy tolerance of the mediocre. They have found . . . suburban or small town life . . . lacking in adventures of the mind and . . . preoccupied with the cultivation of the body and the material assets accruing to members of an inchoate and indeterminate society. They have tended, therefore, to emphasise the themes of isolation and alienation which, although prominent in much Western literature, take on a local and specialised meaning in countries where the writer is more than usually conscious of the absence of a cultural context. Under various guises "Man Alone," to use the title of John Mulgan's novel, has remained a familiar figure in the imaginative prose of New Zealand and, whether he appears in a small town setting or escapes to the silence of the bush, his vague search for a congenial environment is rarely accomplished.[13]

Feminism

In the 1960s and 1970s, a strong feminist movement (by no means the first) in both Australia and New Zealand helped produce and support the appearance of novels and story collections about women.

Some of these portrayed loneliness, at times exploited, by men, as in Phyllis Gant's *The Fifth Season* (1976), Colin Gibson's *The Love Keeper* (1970), or Margaret Jeffrey's *Cabin at Your Gate* (1973). Patricia Grace's *Mutuwhenua* (1978) presents difficulties in the marriage of a Maori woman, Linda, to a Pakeha. On the other hand, in Gibson's fantasy novel *The Pepper Tree* (1971), a young woman known as "The Smart" proves to be not victim but heroine-manager. Social taboos of colonial times are part of the background in G. J. Scrimgeour's *A Woman of Her Times* (1982) and form virtually the whole background in Ivy Hutchinson's *Forbidden Marriage* (1971). In Fiona Kidman's *A Breed of Woman* (1979), the New Zealand career of Harriet Wallace, from girlhood into middle age, covers a wide range of personal experience, sexual and otherwise, from which she emerges as a worn but not yet beaten survivor.

Moving closer to our times, Margaret Sutherland's *The Fledgling* (1974) gives careful attention to the inner life of the heroine, Clodagh, who outwardly is unprepossessing, and in *The Love Contract* (1976) she explores the values and vicissitudes of marriage. Kidman's *Mandarin Summer* (1981) focuses upon a short span of time in 1946, during which a newly widowed woman and her eleven-year old daughter move to the Northland expecting a new and better life but become entangled in a local family feud. Of Jean Watson, whose work also relates to this group, a fellow novelist Marilyn Duckworth has written: "The loneliness of nuclear family life can extend to rural areas too, as Jean Watson makes very clear."[14] *The Godmothers* (1982) by Sandi Hall operates in "aftertime" as well as in the present (in which women are opposing Big Business in Toronto). Titles such as *Odd Woman Out* (Wendy Simons, 1980) or *Four Women* (Jane Wordsworth, 1972) are explicit signals to the reader. Bitter rebellion underlies Ian Wedde's *Dick Seddon's Great Dive* (1976). It goes without saying that both the movement itself and its fictional results owe a great deal to the long-sustained career of Janet Frame.

With Guns in Their Hands

The crime rate in New Zealand is not inordinately high, but neither is violence, including assault and murder, altogether unknown. Probably the most notable murder story (in fact, quasi murder) in New Zealand fiction (leaving aside Ngaio Marsh's books as a special genre) is John Mulgan's *Man Alone* (1939), which was discussed in Chapter 4. This novel, as already noted, was intended by Mulgan to have been called "Talking of War," and it is not unusual to find violence in New Zealand fiction associated, if not directly with war itself, with war veterans. Talking of war explicitly, J. C. Reid notes that there is a small amount of war fiction per se in view of the number of New Zealanders who soldiered in two world wars; he estimates that the Maori wars have generated about three times as many novels as have European wars. From this small number,

. . . the picture that emerges of the New Zealand soldier corresponds to the Kiwi's rather flattering image of himself—tough, laconic, good-natured, self-reliant (unlike those Poms [Englishmen] who always have to be told what to do!), always ready for a fight yet not provoking one. In essence, he is serious-minded under his easy-going exterior. He doesn't like war; but only Davin and Lee get really excited about it. For the others, it is a dirty job to be done, which the Kiwi prides himself he does as well as anyone, even if he'd rather be in the boozer. . . . In other words, when the New Zealand novelist gets beyond the pragmatic, the documentary and the propagandist, it is not to try to glamorise war or to transform it into a nostalgic memory, but to view it as a barometer of man's moral and emotional nature.

Thus, war fiction from New Zealand may be seen as "another index to the underlying strain in the New Zealand consciousness."[15] A later crop of novels in which various crimes are examined with some seriousness includes five novels in the roughly 20-year period between 1949 and 1967: Eric de Mauny, *The Huntsman in His Career* (1949), Guthrie Wilson, *Brave Company* (1951) and *The Feared and the Fearless* (1954), Gordon Slatter, *A Gun in My Hand* (1959), Maurice Gee, *The Big Season* (1962), and Ray Grover, *Another Man's Role* (1967). The first of these is a story of World War II days in which young Gerald Milson, a "quiet" type, kills a salesman whose actions remind him of his father whom he hates. A third man, a young soldier named Peter Villiers who is part of the manhunt for Milson, completes a trio, all of whom are bruised or burnt personalities.

Wilson's book describes a Captain Markham Faulkner who, wounded and discharged from active duty, makes his way to northern Italy and sets up as the partisan leader "Il Brutto," logical, intelligent, but a completely violent man, a type that has proliferated alarmingly since World War II and its chain reaction of smaller wars over the three decades following. Upon his return to New Zealand, he goes berserk and must be hunted down and shot. *Landfall*'s reviewer felt that the treatment of violence was "dangerously irresponsible," since what emerges is "a mystique of violence, as confused and contradictory as such an attitude is likely to be."[16] Reid thinks *Brave Company,* as compared both with this novel and with Davin's *For the Rest of Our Lives* (1947)—"written largely from the officer-caste point of view"—is "more typically Kiwi."[17]

Slatter's hero, ex-soldier Ronald Sefton, carries a gun during a twenty-four-hour stay in Christchurch looking for the man who stole his sweetheart and moving through a panoramic treatment of sports, booze, and mateship with a final decision not to shoot. *The Big Season* is devoted similarly to sports (especially football) and booze, with a fair bit of masculine fighting and a jail sentence for robbery which brings only more trouble with the Auckland police when protested. Gee's *A Special Flower* (1965) is a story of domestic difficulties. Finally, Grover's *Another Man's Role* sends Con Bartlett from the timber country to the Korean War, where he meets Kazuko, a bargirl who gives him sympathy and, gradually, a less belligerent attitude. Upon returning to New Zealand and a job in the mill, he kills a man who insults Kazuko's picture. Another love story set against the Korean War background appears in E. E. Coumbe's *The Cold Noon of Spring* (1965). Jim Henderson's *Gunner Inglorious* (1945–74) consists of brief sketches—the material for a novel about World War II rather than the actual performance itself.

Counterculturists

In 1960, a critic, R. A. Copland, commenting on the hero, young Robbie, of Ian Cross's novel *The Backward Sex,* sees the boy as an exemplar of the "new picaro" with a moral confusion as his whole inward existence: "Life breaks down into physical phenomena and yet sensitivity does flit detached and baffled among them." Despite his machismo, Robbie does have "such delicacies of sense that we occasionally see him to be of finer clay than he himself believes."[18] This might well be taken as the premonitory sign of something astir in the young, although some years of the "silent generation" were to pass before the counterculture, so-called, was to appear in full swing: protest meetings, marches, manifestos, seizures and/or destruction of symbolic official property, sit-ins, teach-ins, draft-card or flag burnings, student strikes, snowstorms and whole blizzards of paper in petitions, leaflets, mushrooming newspapers and youth magazines, heavy emphasis on the generation gap and the credibility gap, new cults and resuscitations of old cults (including witchcraft), male-female egalitarianism (or what was said to be), communes, voluntary poverty and contrivedly conspicuous vagrancy, psychedelic drugs, costumes, posters—all the innumerable antimilitary, antiauthoritarianism, anti-industrial-commercial-political-educational establishment gestures still fresh in our minds. The "new picaro" multiplied like the mushrooms through the use of which, he often believed, inspiration might be induced from extrasensory sources.

Before taking up two writers of this era whose work was sustained beyond one or two novels (Shadbolt and Morrieson), let us sample the years 1965–80 with an eye to novels that show the response to the times on the part of some at least (probably not all) who were themselves involved—though we must not assume that because a novelist writes about events he is necessarily part of them or even sympathetic to them. The first of these, *Stand in the Rain* (1965) by Jean Watson, is short, a 150-page novella, as in fact most of the remainder are. Its central figure and narrator, Sarah, goes to university as a representative counterculturist of the sixties: antiintellectual, uncommitted, hedonistic, mobile. But she meets a young bushman, Abungus, whose marriage has just broken up, and the two settle into more or less conventional domesticity when he becomes a rabbiter in the Wairarapa country north of Wellington. Rain is used symbolically, almost in the sense of "right as rain," to suggest important happenings or a sense of companionship. Catherine McLeod's *Fortunately There Was a Haystack* (1970) takes a comparatively humorous view of the times but remains firmly on the youthful side. Charmian Price, young daughter of North Shore (Auckland) parents, writes a "modern" novel which profoundly shocks her parents when they find the manuscript in her room. They take her to a psychiatrist, Dr. Ropff, whose sessions form part of the story. Charmian's book is accepted for publication; meanwhile, her mother is having an affair with a neighbor, Dr. Milligram. The book is a *succès-de-scandale* when published, but Charmian—who at length marries the psychiatrist—doubts she will write another, even though her mother now wants her to: the psychiatry, plus the psychiatrist himself, has rendered her artistically impotent or at least indifferent. The book "was a way of seeing," and Toby (her husband) "took it away from me" and "replaced it," she explains.[19]

Next, John Hooker in *Jacob's Season* (1971) shows some of the stylistic effects of the time: fragmentary prose highlighted with rhyme, bits of folklore, and popular culture. Jacob Small, unsuccessful in business and confused in judgment, muddles about with sexual infatuations and finally loses all—sweethearts and family. The novel gives us a vivid picture of a quick-witted, life-loving, affectionate extrovert who seems never to reach maturity and, as a result, brings unhappiness to those he loves. The form and style of the book suggest, in themselves, Jacob's confusions. Two other novels from 1971, Nicholas Armfelt's *Catching Up* and Colin Gibson's *The Pepper Leaf,* deal with a man (teacher)-girl (student) involvement and an immediately futurist world, respectively. In the second, the climactic mood is developed through language such as this:

> In every eye could be seen the unconcealed spark of destruction, anarchy, murder—the result of minds too filled with prudence, with reason and its material "civilized" corollaries, and which had led to a frightful dehumanization and impoverishment of life. . . .
>
> Now suddenly there was something to think of with real eagerness, as though in the form of the "savage" before them was embodied a sacred sense of beyond, or timelessness, of a world which had an eternal value and the substance of which was divine.[20]

Michael Henderson's *The Log of a Superfluous Son* (1975)—praised for its economy of style and for the author's "ability to cut right through to the reader, without all the spelt-out verbal and symbolic connexions by his swinging and more intuitive line"[21]—is a rebellious-young-man story in which disillusion reigns supreme. Convinced that everything is besmirched, Osgar Senney (who has been successful enough by conventional standards: he became speechwriter to the prime minister) chooses to be a manure scooper on a cattle boat to Korea rather than continue with the life pattern he has followed in New Zealand. (Is the novelist asking us, symbolically, whether the two occupations are all that dissimilar?)

Finally, to return briefly to matters of form (as touched on in the account of Hooker's *Jacob's Season*), a more recent novel by Michael Harlow, *Nothing but Switzerland and Lemonade* (1980), is a venture into semifiction, semipoetry. Dealing in shifting "texts" to which character and event are loosely attached, the narrative arrives at a sort of fictional surrealism.

Maurice Shadbolt (b. 1932), whose earlier works beginning with *The New Zealanders* (1959) and continuing in *Summer Fires and Winter Country* (1963) were short stories showing a variety of moods and subjects, has proved to be a writer responsive to current culture and as such, a portrayer of events in the role of observer. *Among the Cinders* (1965), his first full-length novel, enters the world of the young through Nick Feinders (narrator), a sixteen-year-old who tells his story to Shadbolt (who thus becomes a character in his own book). Nick leaves home, makes acquaintances among the Auckland University set, and lives with his grandparents, thus gaining a good bit of experience but a dubious "maturity" if any. In *The Presence of Music* (1967), the first of three novellas introduces university people and topics of conversation as part of its background; nothing in the book, however, is particularly countercultural, which might be said as well of *This Summer's Dolphin* (1969) and *An Ear of the Dragon* (1971), although some of the characters are battered souls. *A Touch of Clay* (1974), on the other hand, is resolutely so: about the central figure Pike, a potter in Auckland, revolve an ex-wife, a mistress (young Irene, who has lived and occasionally still does live in a commune), Daniels the commune's leader (who challenges Pike's control over Irene by vilifying her), and others. Irene dies from too many drugs, and Pike is left to brood about life. *Danger Zone* (1975) sends four men on a protest yacht into the French nuclear test zone in the Southwest Pacific.

From all this, it is evident that one of the more prominent New Zealand novelists, now somewhere near the peak of his career, has given more than passing notice to the trends of his times. The final writer of the group, Ronald Hugh Morrieson (1922–1972), was even more intimately involved.

Morrieson's novels are Taranaki's—the North Island's—answer to Janet Frame in a bizarre kind of way. Whereas she makes her agonies serious ones, increasingly insistent, his are comic, but the unvarnished view of New Zealand emerges none the less clearly for that. The Bergsonian interpretation of the comic—that comedy is eternally needful to keep society from becoming immovably rigid and moribund—applies with special force to New Zealand and, indeed, might be shown to have been sporadically illustrated. Humorous writers range from Butler and Maning through Anthony to Barry Crump and Morrieson, not to mention the appearance of humor in verse (as in Crosby Ward, Fairburn, Curnow, Glover, and others). What E. H. McCormick says of Henry Lapham's *We Four* could be readily applied to Morrieson: "The yarns are set down in free colloquial English, they

are spiced with salty male humour and sweetened with that genuine
sentiment which grew out of the stresses of life."[22] And *We Four*, it
happens, was published in 1880!

The story of Ronald Hugh Morrieson reads like a novel in itself,
one of the kind that are hard to believe. He lived in the same house
in the same small town (Hawera) in Taranaki (a cow-cocky, or dairy-
farming, section long synonymous in New Zealand parlance with the
boondocks) all his life, which ended at fifty chiefly by reason of alcoholism. He died at a time when his reputation was barely beginning
to rise, and it is something of an accident that his work ever strug-
gled into print.

The Scarecrow (1964) is a story of minor and major violence told by
Neddy Poindexter, son of the junkman in Klynham, a small town in
or near Taranaki. The Poindexters are a lower-class family with a
good-looking daughter, Prudence; Neddy is well acquainted with
boys from similar families in the town. For a time, trifling juvenile
gang fights and chicken-stealing episodes are comically rendered.
Early in the book, however, we are made aware of another presence:

Although there had been no steady rain, no downpour, for over a week,
there was a big puddle of water in the middle of Klynham's main street. It
was always there, even in the heart of summer. It was a feature of the town.
It had nothing to do with rain, but owed its existence to subterranean
forces, seepage, impermeable strata and so on. The puddle was right outside
the Federal Hotel and had been the looking-glass of many dissolute visages,
many coyly lopsided moons. One night when the wide street was empty and
the moon shepherded a few dark clouds from well aloft the puddle gave to
an evil face a setting of jewels and muddy mountains. The face was owned
by a phenomenally tall man and the devil himself could not have conspired
with a street lamp to cast a longer shadow. It was also the face of a phenomenally thirsty man. A tongue flicked parched lips, eyes sought in vain for a
chink of light, some flaw in the armour of the Federal Hotel. He began to
cross the road. The puddle, automatically skirted, faithfully recorded his
stealthy, purposeful passing.[23]

This is Hubert Salter, the "Scarecrow," magician-villain of the piece.
He remains darkly on the fringes until near the end, when he is involved with the rape-murder of Prudence's friend Angela and an attempt on Prudence herself. Comedy and tragedy walk hand in hand
through Morrieson's pages; Neddy's narrative style is chatty and

slangy, tuned to a careful pitch despite its apparent juvenile license—
a very good vehicle, remaining close to the concrete with only an occasional flash of metaphor, giving the illusion of being not always the
literal transcript of juvenile speech and thinking. The dialogue is
similarly skillful, including several drunk scenes. Parallels in earlier
New Zealand writing are not altogether lacking; M. H. Holcroft, for
instance, sees Reg Jones of *Any Old Dollars, Mister?* (Norman B.
Harvey, 1964, a novel set against the "American invasion" of New
Zealand during the early years of World War II) as related to Neddy.
Holcroft gives Morrieson's novel a good hearing and, though not entirely sympathetic with either its style or content, is one of the earliest and the few to do so in New Zealand.

The darker side of The *Scarecrow* is not really the Scarecrow himself, the
psychopathic killer, a figure of melodrama not to be taken seriously, even in
the climax—as breathless as anything in a silent film—when Prudence is in
danger of losing life and virtue together. The real shadow comes from the
Lynch gang, especially when they try to bully Neddy into taking Prudence
to their hideout, where obviously she is to be raped. One feels in this part
of the book a pressure from outside, a reminder of the sex crimes which in
recent years have occurred rather more often than in the past—mainly, I
think, because the wild boys all drive motor cars nowadays, their own or
somebody else's, so that the street corner of a simpler time has become
mobile.[24]

Came a Hot Friday (also 1964) seems rather brittle in comparison
with *The Scarecrow*. It is a folktale with an ad hoc plot well laced with
rum, gambling, and fast driving over slow roads. Perhaps, at this
point, to Morrieson as to the narrator, "Boyhood can seem a long way
off and so can breakfast."[25] But it evokes the same atmosphere—it
had to, because that is all Morrieson ever knew—of a run-down New
Zealand small town:

It was pleasant enough in the lane, but when one had passed the monu-
ment with all the names of the soldiers who had been rubbed out in a scrap
with the Hau Hau chief Titokowaru, and began walking from overgrown
sleeper to sleeper along the old railway track towards the Von Tempsky
[Hotel], the rot set in. Four of the six shops on the left were shut. Such
curtains as did hang at the upstairs windows were, for the main part, a dis-
grace. The weatherboards of the buildings were grey and blistered. . . . An

empty shop window was full of brown and yellow newspaper. The verandas of this shop and the next, teetering on their supports, provided the only shade in the whole street. The thin patch-work of the footpath ahead was sun-soaked and weed-pierced. A dissolute-looking unshaven man with a bandaged hand leaned against the wall in the shade of the tumbledown verandas.[26]

Predicament (1974, the first of Morrieson's books to be published in New Zealand, where virtually no critical attention was paid him until 1971) rides on a blackmail scheme in which another juvenile principal, Cedric, becomes somewhat reluctantly involved. Unsavory characters like the Spook and Cedric's friend Mervyn Toebeck are at one end of the economic spectrum, and the wealthy young sport Blair Bramwell is at the other, though he is equally unsavory. Cedric's eccentric father and the odd-shaped tower built at the old family mansion offer what appears to be only extra atmosphere, but they too are involved in climactic events. As in *Came a Hot Friday,* serious crime is shown to be riddled with pitfalls; justice, in the end, is not mocked. *Pallet on the Floor* (1976) contains much of the violence of the three earlier novels but lacks their redemptive inlay of comedy.

A prefatory tribute to Morrieson by Maurice Shadbolt terms him "by far our most original writer," one who "certainly takes first place in our eccentric tradition." Of even more interest is Morrieson's own comment on his work:

I have these majestic themes in my mind, you see, big things, shapes like music, but the trouble is getting the characters to fit. I mean, they're not up to the themes; they just turn out funny. So what do I have to do? I just have to make the best of it.[27]

Writers such as Morrieson are treated, often enough, in Clough's ironic words: "Thou shalt not kill but needst not strive/Officiously to keep alive." But among his chief defenders are to be found two of New Zealand's best-known novelists, Sargeson and Shadbolt, along with a prominent critic and poet, C. K. Stead. He could not have written in the counterculturist vein deliberately or even consciously, because he had no acquaintance with the urban centers that generated it; at the same time, comic romancer that he thought himself to be, he shows himself aware of a growing social crisis which radiated into suburbia and even the backblocks of Taranaki, a "what the hell" mood among the young and lately young that easily bred violence and sudden death. Taking what his world gave him, he constructed out of such materials a grotesque realm of his own in as unlikely a place, shall we say, as Wuthering Heights or Hannibal, Missouri.

Some twenty-five years ago, Robert Chapman published in *Landfall* an essay, "Fiction and the Social Pattern," in which he surveyed a number of New Zealand social patterns as seen through novels and stories up to that time: the work ethic, loneliness, violence, dislocations in family life (especially the wide generation gaps and the excessive strains upon women), pressures for conformity, and the like. Each individual author of such fiction, he says, "is driven to be his own sociologist, patiently observing the unrecognized majority pattern as well as the minor variations of which there will be all too few."[28] There is a great deal in Mr. Chapman's essay that points clearly in the direction of the fiction subsequent to his analysis. On the continuing mood of "rebellion" among writers of that time, he observes:

Rebellion against the failures of our pattern is too frequently dismissed, in advance, as rebellion against an idealized statement of how each institution ought to work. That is, the rebel is accused of rebelling against what he agrees with because he points out and rebels against the fact that institutions are working in a different direction and in a worse fashion. The continuing rebel is our rarest product, for the reasons outlined earlier, and his news from outside, presented as art, is worth intelligent consideration.

Certainly the writers who continue to write continue to rebel. They concern themselves, moreover, with figures of rebellion, with men alone, with the occasional violent outbursts of individuals striking blindly against the symbols of authority, with the young coming to awareness and taking sides against their surroundings, with the lost or venturesome few against the many.[29]

A late example of Chapman's thesis on authority, violence, and rebellion may be seen in Edith Campion's *The Chain* (1979), which contains, principally, the interior monologue of a man inexplicably chained to a tree in the New Zealand bush.

Having been through the wringer, more or less, with the dislocations of the 1960s and 1970s, let us turn back to the calm days of the 1950s, to the silent generation, to learn how fiction *should* have been written if A. R. D. Fairburn is a reliable guide. His "Sketch-Plan for

the Great New Zealand Novel" appearing first in *Parsons Packet*,
1950, commences in these words:

> The story is about Tom Shaughnessy, son of an Irish remittance man who
> died fighting in an insane asylum six months before our hero was born, and
> a beautiful young girl of seventeen, an inmate of the Borstal institution.
> Tom has a childhood in which sunshine and shadow are mingled. He forms
> a passionate attachment for his mother, which is to dominate his life. Leav-
> ing school at the age of eighteen, after he has finished for good and all with
> Standard Two, Tom digs post-holes, acts as chucker-out in a tough joint,
> becomes a jockey but is unsuccessful owing to his shortness of stature, writes
> short stories, takes to shop-lifting and serves several gaol sentences (during
> which he makes many new friends), and in general kicks around and is
> kicked around. As can be seen already, Tom Shaughnessy is an ordinary,
> simple New Zealander with the dreams and hopes, the tastes and ambitions,
> of simple, ordinary people.[30]

Following in outline form the remainder of Tom's simple and un-
eventful but wholesome and satisfying career, we learn that he lives
with a missionary's wife who turns out to be a man dressed up as a
woman; is arrested and tried for murder; tries to commit suicide; is
nursed by Hobson Street Hattie (at which point he begins a novel but
"abandons it in despair when he finds that Hattie too is working on
a novel, and that there is nobody to cook the meals"); goes rural on
a sheep farm; and goes to war in the navy. After the war a petty of-
ficer becomes a missionary and Tom lives with him disguised as a
woman; together, they "befriend a shy young man of Irish extraction
named Shawn Tomassey, who is ambitious to become a writer. Shawn
comes to live with them. And so the story ends, with everybody sad-
der and wiser, but looking forward bravely to the future." The author
insists that his story is an "unforgettable picture" of New Zealand
but also "universal"; it "gives us New Zealanders a penetrating study
of us as we really are, beneath our shy exteriors."[31] What shall we
say—that Fairburn was a critic born twenty years too soon?
    Following Fairburn's lead but restricting himself to the short story
(which will be treated at some length in the following chapter),
A. K. Grant in "An Enquiry into the Construction and Classification
of the New Zealand Short Story,"[32] emerges with half a dozen "basic,
irreducible types" which include "the sensitive Maori kid who doesn't
quite know what is going on," "the Ordinary Kiwi working bloke,"
the type who tells the reader "Then if you think you're depressed al-

ready just wait till you read this but it may help me make some sense of my breakdown," "the loveable housewife and mother coping with adolescent kids in the suburbs," "the zonked out of one's skull in Ponsonby" (which "was developed in the sixties" and "attempts to combine the described sexual and hallucinogenic experience without making sense of either and using words rather than language"), and "the sub-Katherine Mansfield 'At the Bay.' " These loose-hung categories, Grant probably would be willing to concede, may at times hybridize—or if they haven't already done so they undoubtedly will.

Chapter Seven
Persistencies

The kitchen clock, the old one that belonged to her grandfather, ticks
with a nobbly loudness, staring with its blank dark eye where you put the
key to wind it. The front of the clock opens and inside are kept for safety,
receipts and bills, art union tickets, and all things that must never be lost
or the Withers will be up before the court or bankrupt.
Yet the clock is time, and time is lost, is bankrupt before it begins.

—Janet Frame, *Owls Do Cry,* 1957

A redemptive value in Maori character, expressed not only in individual
temperament but in family life and *mores,* may be in part, but only in part,
the wistful suppositions of a Pakeha, seeking in another race a wisdom he
despairs of in his own. Something of the kind exists, as every New Zealander knows, and some have proved in experience: a capability for living,
with oneself and with others; a better evaluation of common pleasures and
pains, of poverty or affluence. It is often enough spoken about ignorantly
and sometimes derisively, but even then (one suspects) enviously.

—Allen Curnow, 1975

Despite the anarchic tendencies of the counterculturists in the last
chapter and the concluding joyride with Messrs. Fairburn and Grant,
it is possible to see New Zealand fiction as still essentially a contin-
uum. In this chapter the effort to do so will be made through, first,
a brief survey of the short story; next, an account of recent work by
some of the established novelists; and finally, a series of comparisons
between mainly new writers on four familiar themes: rural life, expatriation, ideas in fictional guise, and pioneering hardship.

The New Zealand Short Story

Supply, in New Zealand writing, has generally exceeded demand.
That is true of the short story as well as the novel—more so than in
Canada, Australia, or the United States with greater potential audi-
ences. Katherine Mansfield, from whom much within the modern
short story in English derives, worked in Europe apart from any di-

rect contact with other New Zealand writers or with the reading public there. So did Jane Mander, in her most creative years. Almost no professional writers with staying power seemed able to develop in New Zealand itself until after World War II, as the short story collections may demonstrate.

Tales by New Zealanders (1938), edited in England by the novelist C. R. Allen, contains stories of merit by twenty-five or so writers. Half a dozen are about Maoris, one or two on historical themes, others on farm life, love, occasional violence, or the problems of youth. Some are more character sketch than narrative. The most noticeable fact about the book is that not very many of the writers are at all known today; most of them were amateurs who for one reason or another did not keep writing. By contrast, a paperback collection of fifteen stories printed in New Zealand on perishable wartime stock in 1945, *Speaking for Ourselves,* edited by Frank Sargeson, contains the work of three writers who had already published collections of stories (Finlayson, G. R. Gilbert, and Sargeson himself) and of five others who would do so later: David Ballantyne, John Reece Cole, Maurice Duggan, A. P. Gaskell, and Helen Shaw. Not only was Sargeson active in promoting the publication of other writers' work, he had helped to bring much of it into being, as H. W. Rhodes points out:

Sargeson's experiments with language, his recognition that the New Zealand vernacular was an appropriate instrument for rendering a New Zealand situation or character, his rigorous exclusion of unnecessary detail and all "literary" flourishes, his attempts to penetrate behind the counterfeit presentation to the moral reality and social significance of an incident without tampering with the truth of his perceptions, together with his close attention to arrangement and narrator's angle of vision, had played their parts in establishing a tradition of short story writing in New Zealand which helped to release new energies and encourage new departures in a number of writers.[1]

The content of the stories in Sargeson's anthology is first of all war talk and returning war veterans, then Maori life, childhood, school, parents and children, gossip, sex, unrecognized talent, work, and death. Sargeson's editorial foreword finds it "surely quite remarkable" that so many writers could be found in New Zealand achieving "a decent competence in the art of short story writing" (presumably something more than the ability to write "tales" as in Allen's 1938 collection). He refers briefly to the *New Zealand Listener,* in which two of the stories first appeared, and probably took it for granted that readers already knew how much state radio had done, both by broadcasting and printing stories, to keep interest alive and writers writing.

Just short of ten years later, Dan Davin's *New Zealand Short Stories* (1953) included twice as many authors, nine of them from the Sargeson volume plus newcomers such as James Courage, Davin himself, Janet Frame (quite early recognition), O. E. Middleton, and Phillip Wilson. There were half a dozen other figures before Katherine Mansfield—a thoroughgoing historical sweep—and from K. M. herself, three stories ("At the Bay," "The Voyage," and "Her First Ball"). The establishment of *Landfall* in 1947 evidently had been almost immediately influential; several stories in Davin's collection had first been published there. By this time, then, it was clear that the short story was a well-recognized form with a growing number of practitioners. Some of these have already been discussed; a few others will be mentioned here.

Maurice Duggan's *Immanuel's Land* (1957) was greeted by *Landfall* with good marks for technique, especially structure: the author was "already a highly accomplished writer" but his stories still were not quite up to the best modern American ones, and he needed "to venture further into the contemporary New Zealand scene."[2] At about the same time, a collection of eleven stories by Helen Shaw, *The Orange Tree* (1957), took its material entirely from the past—portraits of people, houses, and the like. The title story was the only one concerned with Maoris; most of the others were about women characters, old and young. O. E. Middleton, on the other hand, undertook a wide range of times and scenes in his two collections, *The Stone* (1959) and *A Walk on the Beach* (1964). M. H. Holcroft, observing that "the Huckleberry Finn tradition is dispersed in our fiction," finds the stories of Middleton especially good because his juveniles are shown "at full stretch among boyhood interests":

If a boy in one of his stories goes with his elders on a pig hunt, the episode is seen as a boy would see it—the right things emphasized, the casual and faintly proud treatment of violence, the bare and yet faithful etching of background. Everything is restrained by an economical use of words, a style influenced by French literature, and in its own way as effective under our hills and in the open air as it has always been in the streets and cafés and bedrooms of Paris.[3]

Of Duggan, a later critic (C. K. Stead in the introduction to Duggan's *Collected Stories,* 1981) was to write some years following the author's premature death:

> "Language is humanity." No New Zealand writer has been more conscious of this, or more conscious that he worked in a frontier society where language and humanity were in danger of atrophying together.

Collections of stories by other recent authors include Renato Amato's *The Full Circle of the Travelling Cuckoo* (1967, the early death of this author having created widespread regret), David Ballantyne's *And the Glory* (1963), A. P. Gaskell's *The Big Game* (1947), G. R. Gilbert's *Free to Laugh and Dance* (1942), and Phillip Wilson's *Some Are Lucky* (1960).

In 1966, a companion volume, second series, to Davin's collection appeared under the editorship of C. K. Stead, who commented in his introduction: "There is still in New Zealand, as there was in the thirties and forties, evident devotion to the *craft* of the short story, not as a thing in itself, but as a means of getting at the exact flavour, the distinct feel, of our experience."[4] Commenting earlier that "the anthologist is bound to think statistically," Stead draws a numerical comparison between his volume and its predecessor:

> Of the twenty-one writers still living at the time of the publication of D. M. Davin's anthology, only four had published fiction in London. Of the same group, nine have now published there; and of the twenty-one contributors to the present volume, thirteen. . . .
> The contributors to this book have produced altogether about thirty novels, most of them in the last dozen years.[5]

This is some indication of the entire general progress of New Zealand literature in the twenty years since the end of World War II.

Samplings (alphabetically by authors) from half a dozen stories in the second-series volume may reveal some of the extensive range of styles among contemporary writers:

1. A. E. Batistich, "The Gusla"

All through the dinner Simum felt like a man who had strayed into the wrong life. He felt the girls' eyes on him all the time. The neatly placed knives and forks and spoons mocked him with their confusion. Which was

for what? "Ach!" he said aloud, "three forks to have a dinner. Where I come
from one was always enough." He looked up to see Lina and Katie looking
at him with fixed unhappy expressions, so he tried to talk of something else,
but it was just as bad. His English became tangled with the old country
language, as it always did when he was excited, and the guests were
smiling.[6]

2. Marilyn Duckworth, "Loops of Her Hair"
There was once a woman with a low slung bust like a half filled shopping
bag, who came to live in Woolton. Woolton is a slick New Zealand suburb
with lawns and hedges polished by the sun until it resembles an array of
bridal gifts—unused, unusable. The woman, Mrs. Doubleday, could ar-
range flowers artistically, whip up an excellent zabaglione, talk books—even
New Zealand books—and say without hesitation what was dreadful in art
and home decoration.[7]

3. Janet Frame, "The Reservoir"
Our other pastime along the gully was robbing the orchards, but this
summer day the apples were small green hard and hidden by leaves. There
were no couples either. We had the gully to ourselves. We followed the
creek, whacking our sticks, gossiping and singing, but we stopped, immediately silent, when someone—sister or brother—said, "Let's go to the
Reservoir!"
A feeling of dread seized us. We knew, as surely as we knew our names
and our address Thirty-three Stour Street Ohau Otago South Island New
Zealand Southern Hemisphere The World, that we would some day visit the
Reservoir, but the time seemed almost as far away as leaving school, getting
a job, marrying.[8]

4. Olaf Ruhen, "My First Whale"
I suppose I got within thirty yards. It seemed much closer at the time,
and I estimated with some coolness and clarity that the whale was at least
three times the length of the schooner and possessed a greater beam. The
calf was nuzzling under the port flipper, and I was approaching at slow
speed from the port quarter. At thirty yards, as I say, the whale moved.
Without disturbing the calf in the least she turned and faced me, very quietly and deliberately. That was all.
I swung *Alice* around very neatly, I thought, and applied full throttle.[9]

5. Maurice Shadbolt, "The People Before"
If Sunday was often the day when he worked hardest, it was also the best
day for Jim and me, our free day. After morning milking, and breakfast, we
did more or less what we liked. In summer we swam down under the river-
willows; we also had a canoe tied there and sometimes we paddled upriver,

under great limestone bluffs shaggy with toi toi, into country which grew
wilder and wilder. There were huge bearded caves in the bush above the
water which we explored from time to time. There were also big eels to be
fished from the pools of the river.[10]

6. Helen Shaw, "The Bull"

The Valentine's dog stretched itself, rose, and walked round in a circle,
an unforgettable smell wafting up from its body, then it yawned and lay
down, servile nose on its master's boot. Through his binoculars Joseph Valentine watched his daughter retreating into the shrubbery. "There goes a
supporter of lost causes, sir," he said, talking down to the dog and thinking
of the dining room walls that were plastered with Lulu's paintings of water-
falls and pungas. "Pungas! Scatter my ashes over the honest to God tus-
socks, Skipper, and preserve me from the sly, dripping green bush," he
shivered, "though I suppose she enjoys herself, sir," the old man continued,
his voice becoming more charitable as the sun warmed his hands.[11]

A few writers have given up the form (or appear to) and others
have emerged, but none seems at the moment to be quite of the stature of Mansfield or Sargeson. Among those beginning to publish in
the 1970s are Patricia Grace, Philip Mincher, and Margaret Sutherland. Shadbolt (who began with a volume of stories, *The New Zealanders,* in 1959) is a writer of considerable versatility, both in choice
of character or theme, and his stories are "always interesting, even if
they sometimes puzzle and irritate by what seems to be a wilful
blunting of the point or a refusal to unravel enigmas of the human
personality."[12] Finally, we should note the recent appearance of stories (as well as novels, mentioned earlier) by the Maori writer Witi
Ihimaera (*Pounamu, Pounamu,* 1972) and the Samoan writer Albert
Wendt (*Flying-Fox in a Freedom Tree,* 1974). The latter are outstanding for their expression of the Samoan viewpoint, occasionally in Samoan English, as for example:

All this I gone and said are true. It all happen like I say.[13]

Dear reader I had no school—no write no read no number no nothing.
But I a man got big dream, got big everything.[14]

These extracts may be compared with another, describing the climactic moment of "A Resurrection," in which Tala, sorely tempted to
blood revenge for the rape of a sister, struggles with his adopted
Christianity. Entering his enemy's shack by night,

he raised the bushknife. He stopped, the bushknife poised like a crucifix above his head. Mosquitoes stung at the silence with their incessant drone.

"Forgive me," he said to the figure on the bed which, in the gloom, looked like an altar. Carefully, he placed the bushknife across Fetu's paunch, turned, recrossed the threshold and went out into the night and an unwanted sainthood in our scheme of things. [15]

Maori writers, both in Maori and in English, have their own magazine *Te Ao Hou,* which is already a sizable repository of Maori experience.

In such a collection as Manhire's *N.Z. Listener Stories* (1977) one is able to observe stylistic and thematic trends over a whole generation (1941–76) as well as to note differences in the early and late work of Frank Sargeson, the father figure to virtually all modern New Zealand fiction. Sargeson's "Two Worlds" (1941), the opening story, looks back to a time when tension between Catholic and Protestant was almost as strong as it has remained in Belfast. "Making Father Pay" (1975), by contrast, is fantasy-humor. A. P. Gaskell's "The Big Game" (1944) gives us early insight into what has developed steadily as the religion of rugby, seen from inside by one of the players. Maori stories by Roderick Finlayson, Phillip Wilson, and Noel Hilliard (1944, 1958, 1961) predate the appearance of stories about Maoris by Maoris themselves: Witi Ihimaera, Patricia Grace, and the poet Hone Tuwhare (1970, 1973, 1975), with the Samoan writer Albert Wendt appearing in 1964. Since the *Listener,* as it needs to be remembered, is a general-service periodical, not one devoted chiefly to literature, the appearance of writers such as these, with the added presence (two stories) of one of the outstanding fictional stylists New Zealand has produced—Maurice Duggan—as well as of women writers such as Helen Shaw, Janet Frame, and Joy Cowley (two stories), underlines the significance of working arrangements between public broadcasting and private literary art.

Manhire comments, in his preliminary "Notes on the Selection," that "If one were to accept the critical truism that New Zealand authors write well and often about children, one would also have to say that they write as well and as often about the old, the lonely, the emotionally destitute." A second collection by the same editor introduces a number of new names, retaining several from the former collection. In all, the two assemblages provide a generous sampling of a genre represented by upwards of forty authors. Other New Zealand periodicals, notably *Landfall* and *Islands,* would yield similar harvests. Writing in the second of these periodicals during 1977, the critic Lawrence Jones demonstrates that realism, dominant in the New Zealand short story of most of its modern period, continues to be the mode. An account of a three-day seminar on the New Zealand short story, held at Victoria University, Wellington, appears in *Landfall* for June 1979, and the same issue contains an article on women short story writers.

Some Veterans

From what has been said already of Frank Sargeson, the reader will be aware of his position in contemporary New Zealand writing. For a time, he worried critics like M. H. Holcroft (editor of the *New Zealand Listener*) by the sheer dominance of his fictional scene: his work gave the feeling that his

. . . black landscapes and mumbling or voiceless people were being taken as representative, simply because for so long they stood alone near the summit of New Zealand fiction. True, the landscapes of art are not necessarily what we see around us; but I thought we needed more than Sargeson's low-keyed interpretations of life in this country . . . and I feared their influence, both on younger writers and on critical opinion outside—an opinion which, in Britain at least, already rested on assumptions of colonial dumbness.

These feelings disappeared as new writers [e.g., Hilliard, Middleton, Shadbolt, Frame, Ballantyne] moved near him.[16]

Sargeson's *Man of England Now* (1972), containing three novellas (the author's most characteristic form), is a mixture of old and new so far as content is concerned. "I for One" is a reprinted story; "A Game of Hide and Seek" deals with psychological complications, sexual and otherwise, and tends toward black comedy or counterculturist writing. The title story, on the other hand, traces one person, Johnny, from a Lancashire childhood in the early twentieth century through adulthood in rural New Zealand in Depression years to old age in a suburb. Individual sequences, such as the voyage, bush work, and so on, are well developed, and throughout the story Johnny is seen as "a good man, basically peaceful, not concerned with power, not moved by egotism, a man who values the simple pleasures of love and work but does not expect much."[17] *Sunset Village* (1976), set in a pensioners' suburban housing settlement, channels a fine mixture of aging individualists into gallivanting, gossip, romance, and even what looks like a murder. His last novel, *En Route* (1979), is a calculated travesty on New Zealand rural life laced with nymphomania. Interestingly enough, Sargeson began publishing plays during the 1960s, a development arising naturally from his special talents with both situation and dialogue.

Of Dan Davin, who has been one of the steadiest producers of postwar fiction (from a residence in England, with periodic visits to New Zealand), Michael Beveridge observes that his characters are often to be found in transit: "journeys over land, sea and sand, are endemic to his fiction," with the common pattern being "to cast the homestead's offspring among the stranger, or more rarely, as in *No Remittance,* to lead the latter down the road home."[18] Thus, expatriation is still a central concern for Davin as it was for Katherine Mansfield sixty years ago, though it is more muted. The war (which in itself is quite well handled by Davin) is seen as creating circumstances making expatriation not only possible but sometimes probable. In *The Sullen Bell* (1956), for instance, New Zealand war veterans living in London impinge on each other's lives in mutual efforts to heal the scars of war. *Brides of Price* (1972) is set in Oxford (where Davin lives), with trips to the Southwest Pacific by the narrator, Adam Mahon, an anthropologist whose personal story reveals close involvement with five different women during his lifetime. The tenacity of the expatriation motif may be gauged by this comment:

> When the time came for my return to New Zealand, I was glad to go, to waken from this gentle nightmare of estranged identity. I based myself on Auckland and found myself in a new strangeness. I was home and not at home. It became clear to me that to have been an expatriate once was to be one always. Wherever you were. A man is only at home where his past *is*. And the past is a social thing. There must be a company that shares it. But an expatriate has fragmented his past.[19]

Davin is a skilled writer with an easy style that carries a reader along in friendly fashion.

Janet Frame's *Daughter Buffalo* (1973) has movement as well, from New Zealand to New York by the elderly writer Turnlung, whose poetic "Prologue" reveals a readiness for death that suits well enough with New York: he finds the city haunted by death wishes and guilt complexes, especially at a special Death Institute. (One might recall here the earlier views of New York revealed in novels by Jane Mander and Shirley Maddock in Chapter 3.) The book shows the writer to be still very much in the vein she has so long been master of.

Maurice Shadbolt continues to show variety as part of the essential strength of his work, for example, in *This Summer's Dolphin* (1969). In this story, set on Motutangi Island near an imaginary New Zealand city, the arrival of a dolphin to which everyone seems to relate (and as a result begins interrelating with others) is a happy event, but there are human difficulties to complicate matters. The style of this work is mercurial, "changing with the characters themselves and taking the form of letters, newspaper dispatches, diary entries, flickering between past and present tenses, counterpointing its idioms and scenes in the Huxley manner."[20] *Strangers and Journeys* (1972) has a far larger scope, using three generations in four sections: "Fathers" (both on the land and in the city), "Fathers and Sons," "Sons," and "Fathers" again (once sons, whose own sons in turn create problems). It is a vast tome of a book with multiple characters interweaving and much physical violence, but also great gentleness, loyalty, and love. Like the people, the landscape has great beauty but harshness too, presenting a memorable background.

New Writers on Familiar Ground

Expatriation, we have seen, is a continuing subject with Davin; so it is also with two writers whose very different experiences may be compared as a further illustration. Guy Young's *A Country Like Home* (1967, published ten years after its author's death in a Mexican sanitarium, from tuberculosis) is episodic, and fictional only in part. It sketches many different types of North American characters, seeing them "for what they are, not for what he'd like them to be," says K. O. Arvidson, and in doing so, "succeeds where so much literature, and I mean our literature in particular, fails." Arvidson feels that "the liveliest character of all, though least seen by the author, is Young himself."[21] In *Islands* (1973), Phyllis Gant searches the past, particularly her residence in Australia as a girl. She recalls vividly both the scenes and the Australian idiom that serve to set her girlhood experience apart. Her performance, R. A. Copland writes, is possessed of "the rare authenticity that is bestowed by a faithful memory, the mother of all the muses."[22] Part of her recall is a famous British event of the 1930s:

The King loves an American lady. *Is* she a lady? That, it seems like, is the burning question. Of course he should have her. He should be allowed to marry the woman he loves. Look how, when he was Prince of Wales, he

took off his overcoat and gave it to the Welsh miner. They say he wept, seeing how poor the people were. Of course, Baldwin and the rest don't want him King; he'd upset the applecart. He knows too much.
  —If you saw the King pushing Mrs. Simpson in a wheelbarrow, what Melbourne firm would it represent?
  —Search me.
  —Whelan the Wrecker.[23]

The next pair, Nola D. Thompson's *The Sharemilkers* (1966) and Anne Mulcock's *Landscape with Figures* (1971), both deal with rural life. The first is a plain-folks chronicle, narrating the economic progress of a young married couple, Shane and Dilsye Granville, toward self-sufficiency as farmers in rich North Island dairy country. At the end, when they are able to purchase a farm of their own. Dilsye (the narrator) says:

As long as our lives were bound up with the land, the challenge remained. Continual battle against nature, long hours of manual work, frustrations and disappointments; but these would be balanced by the sweet joys of success and the rewarding sense of attainment. . . .
  One thing was certain. This time we were on a farm to stay. We were no longer gipsy farmers.[24]

By contrast, the heroine of *Landscape with Figures,* Hester Carrington, is the middle-aged wife of a wealthy sheep farmer, living a dull life with a husband busy with his farm. A "desperately sad book," Patrick Evans calls it, and for good reasons: Hester is never able to relate to people—husband, daughter, son, or even her former lover, an artist. In this pair of stories we see, well illustrated, the extremes that New Zealand fiction *can* explore, though it must be conceded that the morose, unhappy side of life lands uppermost in more novels than not. So does it elsewhere, no doubt.
  The novel of ideas shown by the third pair—M. K. Joseph's *The Hole in the Zero* (1969) and C. K. Stead's *Smith's Dream* (1971)—is of ancient vintage in New Zealand, going all the way back to Butler's *Erewhon,* Vogel's *A.D. 2000,* and Brown's *Limanora.* Joseph's treatment of the genre is a philosophical plotless narrative, related to science fiction, by a writer whose earliest novel (*I'll Soldier No More,* 1958) was a product of experience in World War II and his second (*A Pound of Saffron,* 1962) of an academic post at Auckland University. (Another more recent novel using an academic character is

Maurice Gee's *In My Father's Den* (1972). In this the hero, an "arty bloke" also from Auckland University, explores both inner and outer worlds, Europe included, in an effort to escape his native puritanism.) *The Hole in the Zero* raises numerous questions, mostly related to the problem of human existence: is it real? Solutions of varying kinds have been sought through individualism, mechanism, Hinduism, in all of which the idea of death-within-life recurs. J. P. Downey, who calls it "a beautiful, subtle, and oblique disquisition on death," says also that it "must be the most cerebral novel yet written by a New Zealander both on the philosophical and on the literary level."[25] *Smith's Dream* is by comparison concrete, offering as it does a futurist situation in which there is a fascist takeover of New Zealand. It is not concrete enough, however, in the opinion of the poet-historian W. H. Oliver, who thinks it fails to show the political process convincingly: the implied question—*could* this happen?—cannot be answered "unless it is suggested that it could have happened in such and such a manner."[26] Both Joseph and Stead, it may be added, are poets, novelists, and critics by turns, not untypical of the range to be encountered among New Zealand writers. Joseph has continued with fantasy in *The Time of Achamoen* (1977). Other blendings of fantasy and politics may be seen in Craig Harrison's *Broken October: New Zealand 1985* (1976), Vincent O'Sullivan's *Miracle* (1976), and John Sligo's *The Cave* (1978).

The final pair, both from the 1970s—James McNeish's *Mackenzie* (1970) and Ian Wedde's *Dick Seddon's Great Dive* (1976)—are different from one another in tone and narrative technique; yet they serve to return us to the themes of search and hardship briefly encountered at the beginning of this study as well as to illustrate the variety that current New Zealand fiction displays. Both are geared to a search for the primordial; both have central characters who in the course of their searching bring suffering and sacrifice upon themselves and others. There is likewise a stark contrast between the searchers' life-styles and those of conventional New Zealand society, although the periods treated are a century apart.

Mackenzie, set in Canterbury (South Island) of the 1860s, divides into two major parts, "The Station" and "The Journey," related yet antithetical. Themes of accident and purpose similarly are intertwined: Mackenzie, for instance, after serving a term in Australia as a boy-convict attempts to migrate to Canada but lands in New Zealand instead. He is a fool-saint figure with a single-minded devotion to his sheep yet deeply religious from boyhood, carrying a Bible as one of his few possessions. He submits calmly and stoically to almost continual exposure and at times incredible hardships; there is a close man-nature bond in him, as shown by his understanding of and reliance upon his dog. As noted in Chapter 1 of this study, he has a sympathetic relationship with the Odessa station owner Amos Polson, who wants Mackenzie to discover and explore new sheep country in order to reserve it for the Maoris (the war in the North Island is taking place at the time of the novel's action). Much of the life of the time is packed into the story: land politics and land-grabber squatters, trips into Christchurch with pictures of the society there, missionary activities among the Maoris, a catastrophic winter blizzard with loss of flocks in the high country and threat to human life, with a constant impression of nature as not being very tractable in this South Island country. Polson's daughter, Frances, also has a natural sympathy with Mackenzie and loyally supports her father's plan. One day as the two of them are out exploring, they stop to look at a river from a height. Here Mackenzie, after musing about the river's long history, discloses a vision of what he takes to be the purpose behind natural processes:

It was the same river had walked with them from the Pacific, he said. It had begun as a fan of shingle. As the plains mounted, it had dug. In the foothills it had cut steps and raised terraces, those barred ramparts above Odessa. Emerging from a ravine, it shed grazing. Whenever it tired of cutting it shed a basin or a delta. The hills were delineated by its skins. As it laboured to reach the alps it deepened, until suddenly it merged pitch with the bluffs of that gorge. It had cut that pass. Breaching the top of the range, it had gathered itself for a final assault, had failed and died. "So I thought, lass. But wait." As he led the dog up, he imagined the land buckling—fissures appearing, to be clothed in forest; crevasses, to be hollowed by the wind and become tarns; the air, steeped in a hail of falling rock. The animals had perished every one, but not the birds. Then the seeds had nurtured on the decaying animals and the grubs had come, all the lizards and insects, in order to feed the birds when they returned famished and out of exile, after first dusting themselves.
    "So thee sees, lass, how the birds had multiplied? The animals has died so the birds shall live."[27]

Dick Seddon's Great Dive takes its "diver"—a young man named Chink as recalled by Kate, who was very much in love with him—into and out of the youth revolution of the 1960s. The title, which underscores Chink's suicide by drowning, uses ironically the name of a flamboyant New Zealand prime minister (1893–1906), perhaps implying that Chink too was, at least in the mind of the woman who adores his memory, in his way a "great man." For Chink, in contrast to Mackenzie, any correspondence between external nature and the realization of his dreams is not immediately apparent. Although on his terms he is as much devoted to nature as Mackenzie was, his life is lived episodically and convulsively, or at least that way insofar as Kate can reconstruct it out of her own painful memory searchings. Kate writes, appropriately to her subject, episodically and convulsively even as her idol lived. Her "large successful scattered middle-class family"[28] are described only enough to establish contrasts and strongly implied conflicts between the establishment and the counterculture during the 1960s in New Zealand as elsewhere. By calling the reader "Wedding Guest" and referring repeatedly to "Xanadu," she borrows both agony and idealization from Coleridge but seems unable or unwilling to parabolize her experience very far past ambivalent sorrow and anger:

A little more yet, Wedding Guest.
I want to ask you a question. That makes you real enough. I mean, I'm expecting an answer.
If I gave you three guesses at what my question is, what would you say? Let *me* guess at those:

1. Do I think my case is so different that it compels you to stay and listen?
2. Do I believe I can expiate (which sounds like spit) by sitting here going through all this?
3. Do I believe it's not too late? or that by starting again I can exclude what's happened?

Give up. For once I'm going to surprise you. *Those* questions stink of formaldehyde. But don't fret, the smell no longer bothers me.
Here's my question. (Here's my stone.)
How do you like my tone?

After some further emotionalizing, she asks still another question, supplying this time a plain enough answer: "Who are you, Wedding Guest? We killed Chink, remember? You're Them."[29] "They," it goes without saying, will not admire her tone, partly at least because it is already dated, exposing its excesses and at the same time its inabilities to mount any really effective opposition. It remains a pathetic tirade.

In novels such as these two, time comes full circle: back to the land in its elemental form, onward to a potentially explosive crisis in the social evolution of its inhabitants. *Mackenzie,* in particular, is a fit novel with which to close the account. It is a monumental effort, by any standard, well able to represent the country of its origin and be judged in the great world fair of World English.

Notes and References

Chapter One

1. *Chambers's Papers for the People* (Edinburgh: W. & R. Chambers, 1870), #85, "New Zealand," p. 31.
2. Mrs. J. E. Aylmer, *Distant Homes; or the Graham Family in New Zealand* (London, 1862), p. 172.
3. Ibid., pp. 196–97.
4. F. E. Maning, *Old New Zealand* (Christchurch, n.d.), pp. 55–56.
5. E. H. McCormick, *Letters and Art in New Zealand* (Wellington, 1940), p. 80.
6. Joan Stevens, *The New Zealand Novel 1860–1960* (Wellington, 1961), p. 15.
7. Phillip Wilson, *William Satchell* (New York: Twayne, 1968), p. 79.
8. Ibid., p. 123.
9. Ibid., p. 135.
10. John C. Reid, *Creative Writing in New Zealand* (Auckland, 1946), p. 48.
11. Stevens, *N.Z. Novel 1860–1960,* p. 26.

Chapter Two

1. Julius Vogel, *A.D. 2000; or, Woman's Destiny,* 3d ed. (Sydney and Brisbane: Edwards, Dunlop & Co., 1890), p. 208.
2. Ibid., pp. 330–31.
3. Elizabeth M. Smith, *A History of New Zealand Fiction* (Wellington: Reed, 1939), p. 31.
4. J. Macmillan Brown [Godfrey Sweven], *Limanora, the Island of Progress* (New York, 1903), pp. 340–41.
5. George Chamier, *A South-Sea Siren,* ed. Joan Stevens (Auckland, 1970), p. 115. (First published 1895.)

Chapter Three

1. *Encyclopedia of New Zealand* (Wellington: Government Printer, 1966), 1:573.
2. Ian Gordon, *Katherine Mansfield,* rev. ed. (London, 1971), pp. 18–19.
3. Ibid., p. 23.
4. *Undiscovered Country: The New Zealand Stories of Katherine Mansfield,* ed. Ian Gordon (London, 1974), p. xxi.
5. Ibid., pp. 30, 354, 231, 213.
6. Antony Alpers, *Katherine Mansfield* (London: Cape, 1954), pp. 192–93.

7. McCormick, *Letters & Art in N.Z.*, p. 135.

8. Dorothea Turner, *Jane Mander* (New York, 1972), p. 38.

9. Jane Mander, *Allen Adair*, ed. Dorothea Turner (Auckland, 1971), p. 134.

10. Ibid., p. 94.

11. Jane Mander, *The Besieging City* (London, 1926), p. 95.

12. Shirley Maddock, *With Gently Smiling Jaws* (Auckland, 1963), p. 42.

13. John C. Reid, *New Zealanders at War in Fiction* (Auckland, 1966), p. 4.

14. Gloria Rawlinson, "Robin Hyde and *The Godwits Fly*," in *Critical Essays on the New Zealand Novel*, ed. Cherry Hankin (Auckland, 1976), p. 42.

15. Iris G. Wilkinson [Robin Hyde], *The Godwits Fly*, ed. Gloria Rawlinson (Auckland, 1970), pp. 172–73. (First published 1938.)

16. R. A. Copland, "The New Zealand Novels of James Courage," *Landfall* 18 (September 1964):249.

17. M. H. Holcroft, *Islands of Innocence: The Childhood Theme in New Zealand Fiction* (Wellington, 1964), p. 53.

18. H. Winston Rhodes, *New Zealand Fiction Since 1945* (Dunedin, N.Z., 1968), p. 20.

Chapter Four

1. F. S. Anthony and Francis Jackson, *Me and Gus* (Wellington: 1951), p. 72. The late Frank Sargeson (in *Islands*, December 1977) paid tribute to Anthony's sketches, remarking that they reveal "the good writing and reading that might be discovered in the use of the New Zealand vernacular."

2. Smith, *History of N.Z. Fiction*, pp. 62–63.

3. Joan Stevens, *The New Zealand Novel, 1860–1965* (Wellington, 1966), p. 45.

4. Stevens, *N.Z. Novel 1860–1960*, p. 44.

5. Ngaio Marsh, *Colour Scheme* (London: Collins, 1964), p. 218.

6. Smith, *History of N.Z. Fiction*, p. 28.

7. Reid, *Creative Writing in N.Z.*, p. 57.

8. E. H. McCormick, *New Zealand Literature: A Survey* (London, 1959), p. 92.

9. P. C. M. Alcock, "A True Colonial Voice: Blanche Edith Baughan," *Landfall* 26, no. 2 (June 1972):165.

10. McCormick, *N.Z. Literature*, p. 91.

11. Alan Mulgan, *Great Days in New Zealand Writing* (Wellington, 1963), p. 96.

12. Nelle M. Scanlan, *Pencarrow* (London, 1932), p. 85.

13. John Guthrie, *The Little Country* (London: Nelson, 1935), p. 103.

14. Bill Pearson, review article on Guthrie, *Landfall* 8, no. 3 (September 1954):227.

15. H. Winston Rhodes, *New Zealand Novels* (Wellington, 1969), p. 41.
16. John A. Lee, *Children of the Poor* (Christchurch: Whitcombe, 1973), p. 16.
17. John A. Lee, *Shiner Slattery* (Auckland, 1964), p. 19.
18. Ibid., p. 13.
19. Denis Glover in *Landfall* 5, no. 2 (June 1951):150.
20. K. O. Arvidson in *Landfall* 19 (March 1965):73. See also Dennis McEldowney's essay on *Children of the Poor* in *Critical Essays,* ed. Hankin, pp. 24–39.
21. Margaret Escott, *Show Down,* ed. Robert Goodman (Auckland, 1973), p. xxv.
22. Ibid., pp. 49–50.
23. Frank Sargeson, *Collected Stories* (Hamilton, N.Z., 1964), p. 15.
24. H. Winston Rhodes, *Frank Sargeson* (New York: Twayne, 1969), pp. 39–40.
25. Sargeson, *Collected Stories,* p. 157.
26. Rhodes, *Frank Sargeson,* p. 45.
27. Paul W. Day, *John Mulgan* (New York: Twayne, 1968), p. 96.
28. Ibid., pp. 120–21.

Chapter Five

1. Stevens, *N.Z. Novel 1860–1960,* p. 77.
2. Bill Pearson, "The Maori and Literature: 1938–1965," in *Essays on New Zealand Literature,* ed. Wystan Curnow (Auckland, 1973), p. 119.
3. Stevens, *N.Z. Novel 1860–1965,* p. 124.
4. Errol Brathwaite, *The Evil Day* (London, 1967), pp. 172–73.
5. Pearson, "The Maori and Literature," in *Essays on N.Z. Literature,* ed. Curnow, p. 117.
6. Anne Holden, *Rata* (Christchurch, 1965), p. 177.
7. Heretaunga Pat Baker, *Behind the Tattooed Face* (Whatamongo Bay, 1975), p. 265.
8. Witi Ihimaera, *Tangi* (Auckland, 1973), p. 349.
9. Ibid., p. 192.
10. H. Winston Rhodes in *Landfall* 29 (June 1975):164.
11. Bill Pearson, review of *Leaves of the Banyan Tree, Islands* 8, no. 2 (June 1980):170.
12. Albert Wendt, *Sons for the Return Home* (Auckland, 1973), p. 203.
13. K. O. Arvidson in *Landfall* 29 (March 1975):75.

Chapter Six

1. M. K. Joseph in *Landfall* 13, no. 2 (June 1959):179.
2. Patricia Guest in *Landfall* 6, no. 2 (June 1952):153.
3. Ibid.

4. H. Winston Rhodes in *Landfall* 11, no. 4 (December 1957):328.

5. Cherry Hankin, "Language as Theme in *Owls Do Cry*," in *Critical Essays*, ed. Hankin, p. 104.

6. Margaret Dalziel, *Janet Frame* (Wellington, 1980), p. 43.

7. Patrick Evans, *Janet Frame* (Boston, 1977), p. 199.

8. Maurice Duggan in *Islands* 3 (1974):333.

9. E. H. McCormick in *Landfall* 12, no. 3 (September 1958):286.

10. Rhodes, *N.Z. Fiction Since 1945*, p. 35.

11. Joy Cowley, *Man of Straw* (London: Secker & Warburg, 1970), pp. 198–99.

12. David Ballantyne, *The Last Pioneer* (London: R. Hale, 1963), pp. 158–159.

13. Rhodes, *N.Z. Fiction Since 1945*, pp. 10–11.

14. Marilyn Duckworth, review of *The World Is an Orange and The Sun, Islands* 7, no. 3 (April 1979):318.

15. Reid, *New Zealanders at War in Fiction*, p. 6.

16. Lawrence Baigent in *Landfall* 8, no. 4 (December 1954):306.

17. Reid, *New Zealanders at War in Fiction*, p. 5.

18. R. A. Copland in *Landfall* 14 (December 1960):397.

19. Catherine McLeod, *Fortunately There Was a Haystack* (Wellington, 1970), p. 132.

20. Colin Gibson, *The Pepper Leaf* (London, 1971), p. 209.

21. L. D. Stayte in *Islands* 4, no. 4 (Summer 1975):473.

22. McCormick, *N.Z. Literature*, p. 60.

23. Ronald Hugh Morrieson, *The Scarecrow* (London, 1964), p. 34.

24. Holcroft, *Islands of Innocence*, p. 41. *New Zealand News U.K.* of September 9, 1982, announced that a NZ film, "The Scarecrow," was in production, with the American actor John Carradine in the title role.

25. Ronald Hugh Morrieson, *Came a Hot Friday* (Sydney, 1964), p. 52.

26. Ibid., pp. 81–82.

27. Maurice Shadbolt in R. H. Morrieson, *Predicament* (Palmerston North, N.Z., 1974), pp. 12, 10.

28. Robert Chapman, "Fiction and the Social Pattern," in *Essays on N.Z. Literature*, ed. Curnow, p. 75.

29. Ibid., pp. 94–95.

30. A. R. D. Fairburn, *The Woman Problem and Other Prose* (Auckland: Paul, 1967), p. 153.

31. Ibid., pp. 154–155.

32. In Bill Manhire, ed., *N.Z. Listener Stories* (Wellington, 1977), pp. 146–49.

Chapter Seven

1. Rhodes, *N.Z. Fiction Since 1945*, p. 23.

2. R. A. Copland in *Landfall* 10, no. 1 (March 1957):79, 80.

3. Holcroft, *Islands of Innocence,* pp. 44–45. See also Dennis Mc-Eldowney's comments in *Landfall,* March 1965.

4. C. K. Stead, ed., *New Zealand Short Stories,* 2d ser. (Wellington, 1966), p. xvii.

5. Ibid., p. xvi.

6. Ibid., pp. 61–62.

7. Ibid., p. 357.

8. Ibid., pp. 177–78.

9. Ibid., pp. 54–55.

10. Ibid., p. 303.

11. Ibid., p. 56.

12. Rhodes, *N.Z. Novel Since 1945,* p. 48.

13. Albert Wendt, *Flying-Fox in a Freedom Tree* (Auckland: 1974), p. 33.

14. Ibid., p. 145.

15. Ibid., p. 71.

16. M. H. Holcroft, *Reluctant Editor* (Wellington, 1969), pp. 112–13.

17. Lawrence Jones in *Islands* 1, no. 2 (Summer 1972):173–74.

18. Michael Beveridge, review of *Not Here, Not Now, Landfall* 24 (September 1970):296.

19. Dan Davin, *Brides of Price* (London, 1972), p. 43.

20. R. A. Copland in *Landfall* 23 (December 1968):407.

21. K. O. Arvidson in *Landfall* 21 (June 1967):206.

22. R. A. Copland in *Landfall* 27, no. 3 (September 1973):259.

23. Phyllis Gant, *Islands* (London, 1973), p. 221.

24. Nola D. Thompson, *The Sharemilkers* (Auckland, 1966), p. 185.

25. J. P. Downey in *Landfall* 23 (March 1969):93.

26. W. H. Oliver in *Islands* 1, no. 2 (Summer 1972):172.

27. James McNeish, *Mackenzie* (London, 1970), pp. 269–70. McNeish's *As for the Godwits* (1977) is a series of personal experiences and observations that a reader might well find interesting as revealing a novelist's responses to life which are viewed as material for fiction. Peter Hooper's *A Song in the Forest* (1979) uses the South Island landscape west to east—the West Coast to the plains of Canterbury—as backdrop to a future primitive world, made so through instant destruction of our civilization by nuclear madness. Readers may readily see parabolic associations between Hooper's story and those of McNeish and Samuel Butler.

28. Ian Wedde, *Dick Seddon's Great Dive, Islands* (Auckland), whole no. 6 (November 1976), p. 174.

29. Ibid., p. 180.

Selected Bibliography

Note: First, a number of still useful anthologies are listed; next, books of literary criticism or general background to the study of New Zealand fiction; then periodicals; and finally, authors and titles of novels and stories in alphabetical order. A date in brackets at the end of an entry indicates the date of original publication.

ANTHOLOGIES

Brasch, Charles, ed. *Landfall Country: Work from 'Landfall,'* 1947–61. Christchurch: Caxton, 1962. Includes twelve short stories.

Catley, Christine Cole, ed. *Shirley Temple Is a Wife and Mother.* Whatamongo Bay, N.Z.: Cape Catley, 1977. Thirty-four stories by twenty-two New Zealand authors.

Davin, D. M., ed. *New Zealand Short Stories.* London: Oxford, 1953. Generally recent authors, but a few as early as the 1870s–80s.

Hill, David, and Smither, Elizabeth, eds. *The Seventies Connection.* Dunedin, N.Z.: McIndoe, 1980. Miscellany of recent New Zealand writing, including selections from the works of numerous writers of fiction, long and short.

Islands (periodical). *Anthology of Contemporary New Zealand Fiction* 3, no. 1 (Autumn 1974). Sixteen authors, with portraits.

————. *Anthology of Short Stories* 4, no. 2 (Winter 1975). Some dozen or more current authors.

Manhire, Bill, ed. *New Zealand Listener Stories.* Wellington: Methuen, 1977. Selected stories published between 1941 and 1976.

————. *New Zealand Listener Stories.* Vol. 2. Wellington: Methuen, 1978.

Meikle, Phoebe, ed. *Short Stories by New Zealanders.* Auckland: Longman Paul, 1970. A study guide, with preface, notes, and questions; includes Frank Sargeson, A. P. Gaskell, Dan Davin, Maurice Duggan.

————. *Short Stories by New Zealanders, Two.* Auckland: Longman Paul, 1972. Authors: Roderick Finlayson, Douglas Stewart, Henry Brennan, A. E. Batistich, David Ballantyne, O. E. Middleton, Renato Amato, Noel Hilliard, Rowley Habib, Witi Ihimaera.

————. *Ten Modern New Zealand Story Writers.* Auckland: Longman Paul, 1976. Authors: Maurice Duggan, Maurice Gee, Patricia Grace, Rowley Habib, Witi Ihimaera, Fiona Kidman, O. E. Middleton, Philip Mincher, C. K. Stead, Margaret Sutherland.

Orbell, Margaret, ed. *Contemporary Maori Writing.* Wellington: Reed, 1970.

O'Sullivan, Vincent, ed. *New Zealand Short Stories, Third Series.* London: Oxford, 1975. New authors: Philip Mincher, Barry Mitcalfe, Owen Leeming, Warren Dibble, Joy Cowley, Patricia Grace, Vincent O'Sullivan, Michael Henderson, Margaret Sutherland, Rachel Bush, Witi Ihimaera.

Reid, J. C., ed. *The Kiwi Laughs: An Anthology of New Zealand Prose Humour.* Wellington: Reed, 1979 [1961].

Stead, C. K., ed. *New Zealand Short Stories, Second Series.* London: Oxford University Press, 1966. New authors: Olaf Ruhen, A. E. Batistich, E. S. Grenfell, Maurice Duggan, Bill Pearson, Terry Sturm, Renato Amato, Noel Hilliard, Maurice Gee, Maurice Shadbolt, C. K. Stead, Alexander Guyan, Marilyn Duckworth.

LITERARY CRITICISM; GENERAL BACKGROUND

Alcock, P. C. M. "On the Edge: New Zealanders as Displaced Persons." *World Literature Written in English* 16, no. 1 (April 1977):127–42. Katherine Mansfield, John Mulgan, Frank Sargeson, Janet Frame.

_____ . "Informing the Void: Initial Cultural Displacement in New Zealand Writing." *Journal of Commonwealth Literature* 6, no. 1 (June 1971):84–102.

Burns, James. *New Zealand Novels and Novelists, 1861–1979, an Annotated Bibliography.* Auckland: Heinemann, 1981.

Curnow, Wystan, ed. *Essays on New Zealand Literature.* Auckland: Heinemann, 1973.

Davin, Dan M., and Davin, W. K. *The New Zealand Novel.* Writing in New Zealand educational series, vol. 10, nos. 1–2. Wellington: Government Printer, 1956.

Dudding, Robin, ed. *Beginnings: New Zealand Writers Tell How They Began Writing.* Wellington: Oxford, 1980. Eleven writers, of whom the majority are novelists or storywriters.

An Encyclopedia of New Zealand. Edited by A. H. McLintock. 3 vols. Wellington: Government Printer, 1966. Contains up-to-date discussions of New Zealand literature.

Evans, Patrick. "Paradise of Slaughterhouse: Some Aspects of New Zealand Proletarian Fiction." *Islands* 8, no. 1 (March 1980):71–85.

Hankin, Cherry, ed. *Critical Essays on the New Zealand Novel.* Auckland: Heinemann, 1976. One novel by each of nine authors selected for intensive discussion: Jane Mander, John A. Lee, Robin Hyde, John Mulgan, Dan Davin, Janet Frame, Bill Pearson, Frank Sargeson, Maurice Shadbolt.

_____ . *Critical Essays on the New Zealand Short Story.* Auckland: Heinemann, 1982.

———. "New Zealand Women Novelists: Their Attitudes toward Life in a Developing Society." *World Literature Written in English* 14, no. 1 (April 1975):144–67.

Holcroft, M. H. *Discovered Isles.* Christchurch: Caxton, 1950.

———. *Islands of Innocence: The Childhood Theme in New Zealand Fiction.* Wellington: Reed, 1964.

———. *Reluctant Editor.* Wellington: Reed, 1969.

Jones, Joseph. "Provincial to International: Southwest Pacific Literature in English since the 1920s." In *Australia, New Zealand, and the Pacific Islands since the First World War.* Edited by William S. Livingston and William Roger Louis. Austin: University of Texas Press, 1979, pp. 125–47. Summary survey.

Jones, Lawrence. "The Persistence of Realism: Dan Davin, Noel Hilliard and Recent New Zealand Short Stories." *Islands* 6, no. 2 (December 1977):182–200. Surveys comprehensively the realistic mode in New Zealand short fiction and makes comparisons with practices in other countries.

Long, D. C. "The New Zealand Literary Magazines." *World Literature Written in English* 14, no. 1 (April 1975):168–74. A useful compilation.

McCormick, E. H. *Letters and Art in New Zealand.* Wellington: Department of Internal Affairs, 1940.

———. *New Zealand Literature.* London: Oxford University Press, 1959. The standard reference, now in need of updating.

Modern Fiction Studies (special issue). *Modern New Zealand and Australian Fiction.* West Lafayette, Ind.: Purdue University, 1981. A dozen articles, some of them extensive surveys, together with useful bibliographies.

Moorehead, Alan. *The Fatal Impact: An Account of the Invasion of the South Pacific, 1767–1840.* London: Penguin, 1968.

Mulgan, Alan. *Great Days in New Zealand Writing.* Wellington: Reed, 1963.

New, William H. *Among Worlds, an Introduction to Modern Commonwealth and South African Fiction.* Erin, Ont.: Press Porcepic, 1975. Chapter on New Zealand, "Escape into Distance," pages 133–56, emphasizes writers since 1950.

———, comp. *Critical Writings on Commonwealth Literatures: A Selective Bibliography to 1970, with a List of Theses and Dissertations.* University Park: Pennsylvania State University Press, 1975. Some twenty-five to thirty writers listed, preceded by general references.

Oliver, W. H. *The Story of New Zealand.* London: Faber, 1960.

Pearson, Bill. *Fretful Sleepers and Other Essays.* Auckland and London: Heinemann, 1974.

Reid, Ian. *Fiction and the Great Depression: Australia and New Zealand, 1930–1950.* Melbourne: E. Arnold, 1979.

Reid, John C. *Creative Writing in New Zealand.* Auckland: published by the author, 1946.

———. *New Zealanders at War in Fiction.* Auckland: New Zealand Publishing Society, 1966. Folded broadsheet.

Rhodes, H. Winston. *New Zealand Fiction Since 1945.* Dunedin, N.Z.: McIndoe, 1968.

———. *New Zealand Novels.* Wellington: New Zealand University Press, 1969. A study guide.

Smith, Elizabeth Maisie. *A History of New Zealand Fiction.* Wellington: Reed, 1939. For its time, quite a good account.

Stevens, Joan. *The New Zealand Novel, 1860–1965.* Wellington: Reed, 1966. A revision and extension of the volume published in 1961.

———. *New Zealand Short Stories.* Wellington: Price Milburn, 1968. Study guide to selected stories by Katherine Mansfield, Frank Sargeson, Janet Frame, and C. K. Stead.

Thomson, John. *New Zealand Literature to 1977: A Guide to Information Sources.* Detroit: Gale Research Co., 1980. "Fiction," pages 34–39, is very useful for references to periodical criticism; individual bibliographies of eighteen novelists and storywriters.

Twayne's World Authors Series. New York and Boston: Twayne Publishers. Volumes on individual authors as indicated in Notes and References.

PERIODICALS

1. International

Ariel. Calgary, Canada, 1970–   . "A Review of International English Literature."

Journal of Commonwealth Literature. London, 1966–   . In addition to articles and reviews, contains selective annual bibliographies of national literatures.

World Literature Today. Norman, Oklahoma, 1927–   . Formerly *Books Abroad;* a pioneering journal of international writing in English and other languages.

World Literature Written in English. Austin and Arlington, Texas, 1962–79; Guelph, Ontario, 1979–   . Articles, reviews, special bibliographies and checklists, interviews.

2. New Zealand and Regional

Islands. Auckland, 1972–   .

Landfall. Christchurch, 1947–   . The oldest journal in New Zealand devoted solely to literature and the arts.

Mate. Wellington, 1957–   .

New Zealand Listener. Wellington, 1939–   . Stories, feature articles, reviews.

Pacific Quarterly. Hamilton, 1978–   . Formerly *Cave* and *New Quarterly Cave;* local and international material; some regional emphasis.

Span. Brisbane, 1975–   . Newsletter of the South Pacific Association for Commonwealth Literature and Language Studies.

AUTHORS AND TITLES

The following list is selective, both as to authors included and works by authors. References to comprehensive lists in author-bibliographies or other special studies are appended when available. Authors and titles discussed in the text appear in this list, as do a number of others. Selected critical references are also included.

Acheson, Frank (1887–1948). *Plume of the Arawas.* London: Dent, 1930. Reprint. Wellington: Reed, 1974.

Adams, Arthur H. (1872–1936). *Tussock Land: A Romance of New Zealand and the Commonwealth.* London: Unwin, 1904.

Allen, C. M. See Escott, Margaret.

Amato, Renato (1928–1964). *The Full Circle of the Travelling Cuckoo* (stories). Christchurch: Whitcombe & Tombs, 1967.

Anthony, Frank S. (1891–1925). *Follow the Call.* Dunedin, N.Z.: Reed, 1936. Reprint. Introduction by T. Sturm. Auckland: Auckland University Press and Oxford University Press, 1975.

Anthony, Frank S., and Jackson, Francis. *Me and Gus.* Wellington: Reed, 1951. Reprint as *Gus Tomlins.* Introduction by T. Sturm. Auckland: Auckland University Press and Oxford University Press, 1977.

Armfelt, Nicholas (b. 1935). *Catching Up.* London: Faber, 1971.

Ashton-Warner, Sylvia. See Henderson, Sylvia Constance.

Audley, E. H. (b. 1895). *Islands Float at Eleven* (sketches). Wellington: Reed, 1952.

———. *A New Gate for Mattie Dulivich.* London: Hodder & Stoughton, 1965.

———. *No Boots for Mr. Moehau.* London: Hodder & Stoughton, 1963.

Aylmer, Mrs. J. E. (?–1908). *Distant Homes; or the Graham Family in New Zealand.* London: Griffith & Farran, 1862.

Baker, Heretaunga Pat. *Behind the Tattooed Face.* Whatamongo Bay: Cape Catley, 1975.

Baker, Louisa A. [Alien] (1858–1926). *A Daughter of the King.* London: Hutchinson, 1894.

Ballantyne, David (b. 1924). *And the Glory* (stories). London: R. Hale; Christchurch: Whitcombe & Tombs, 1963.

————. *The Cunninghams*. Auckland: Whitcombe & Tombs, 1963 [1948].
————. *A Friend of the Family*. London: R. Hale, 1966.
————. *The Last Pioneer*. London: R. Hale, 1963.
————. *The Penfriend*. Palmerston North, N.Z.: Dunmore, 1980.
————. *Sydney Bridge Upside Down*. London: R. Hale, 1968.
Barker, Lady Mary Anne (1831–1911). *A Christmas Cake in Four Quarters*. London: Macmillan, 1871.
Batistich, A. E. (b. 1915). *An Olive Tree in Dalmatia* (stories). Hamilton, N.Z.: Paul's Book Arcade, 1963.
Baughan, Blanche E. (1870–1958). *Brown Bread from a Colonial Oven* (stories). Christchurch: Whitcombe & Tombs, 1912.
Baume, F. E. (1900–67). *Half-Caste*. London: Falcon, 1950.
Bell, John. *In the Shadow of the Bush*. London: Sands, 1899.
Billing, Graham (b. 1936). *The Alpha Trip*. London: W. H. Allen, 1969.
————. *Forbush and the Penguins*. Wellington: Reed, 1965.
————. *The Primal Therapy of Tom Purslane*. Melbourne: Quartet Books, 1980.
————. *The Slipway*. London: Quartet Books, 1974.
————. *Statues*. London: Hodder & Stoughton, 1971. [Interview in *Landfall* 34 (September 1980):249–61.]
Boldrewood, Rolf. See Browne, Thomas Alexander.
Bolitho, Hector (1898–1974). *Solemn Boy*. London: Chatto & Windus, 1927.
Brathwaite, Errol (b. 1924). *An Affair of Men*. New York: St. Martin's, 1961.
————. *The Evil Day*. London: Collins, 1967.
————. *Fear in the Night*. Christchurch: Caxton, 1959.
————. *The Flying Fish*. London: Collins, 1964.
————. *Long Way Home*. Christchurch: Caxton, 1964.
————. *The Needle's Eye*. London and Auckland: Collins, 1965.
Brodie, John [John Guthrie] (1905–55). *The Little Country*. London: Nelson, 1935.
————. *Paradise Bay*. London: W. Laurie, 1952.
————. *The Seekers*. London: W. Laurie, 1952.
————. *So They Began*. London: Nelson, 1936. [Bill Pearson, "John Guthrie," in *Fretful Sleepers and Other Essays* (Auckland and London: Heinemann, 1974), pp. 37–42.]
Brown, J. Macmillan [Godfrey Sweven] (1846–1935). *Limanora, the Island of Progress*. New York: Putnam, 1903.
————. *Riallaro, the Archipelago of Exiles*. New York: Putnam, 1901.
Browne, Thomas Alexander [Rolf Boldrewood] (1826–1915). *War to the Knife, or Tangata Maori*. London: Macmillan, 1899.
Burdon, R. M. (1896–1965). *Outlaw's Progress*. Wellington: Progressive Society, 1943.

Butler, Samuel (1835–1902). *Erewhon.* London: Trubner, 1872.

———. *Erewhon Revisited.* London: Richards, 1901. [Lee E.

Holt, *Samuel Butler* (New York: Twayne Publishers, 1964); Joseph Jones, *The Cradle of Erewhon: Samuel Butler in New Zealand* (Austin: University of Texas Press, 1959); Peter B. Maling, *Samuel Butler at Mesopotamia* (Wellington: Government Printer, 1960).]

Campion, Edith (b. 1923). *The Chain.* Wellington: Reed, 1979.

———. *A Place to Pass Through and Other Stories.* Wellington: Reed, 1977.

Chamier, George (1842–1915). *Philosopher Dick: Adventures and Contemplations of a New Zealand Shepherd.* London: Unwin, 1891.

———. *A South Sea Siren.* Edited and with an introduction by Joan Stevens. Auckland: Auckland University Press and Oxford University Press, 1970 [1895].

Clyde, Constance (1872–   ). *A Pagan's Love.* London: Unwin, 1905.

Cody, J. F. (1895–1967). *The Red Kaka.* Wellington: Reed, 1955.

Cole, John Reece (b. 1916). *It Was So Late* (stories). Christchurch: Caxton, 1949. New edition with an introduction by Cherry Hankin. Auckland: Auckland University Press, 1978.

Courage, James (1903–1963). *The Call Home.* London: Cape, 1956.

———. *Desire without Content.* London: Constable, 1950.

———. *The Fifth Child.* London: Constable, 1948.

———. *Fires in the Distance.* London: Constable, 1952.

———. *Such Separate Creatures* (stories). Christchurch: Caxton, 1973.

———. *A Way of Love.* London: Cape, 1959.

———. *The Young Have Secrets.* London: Cape, 1954.

Cowley, Joy (b. 1936). *The Growing Season.* Garden City, N.Y.: Doubleday, 1978.

———. *The Man of Straw.* London: Secker & Warburg, 1970.

———. *The Mandrake Root.* Garden City, N.Y.: Doubleday, 1975.

———. *Nest in a Falling Tree.* London: Secker & Warburg, 1967.

———. *Of Men and Angels.* Garden City, N.Y.: Doubleday, 1972.

Cross, Ian (b. 1925). *After Anzac Day.* London: Deutsch, 1961.

———. *The Backward Sex.* London: Deutsch, 1960.

———. *The God Boy.* London: Deutsch, 1958; New York: Harcourt Brace, 1958.

Crump, Barry (b. 1935). *The Best of Crump* (stories). Auckland: Crump Productions, 1974.

———. *A Good Keen Man* (stories). Wellington: Reed, 1960.

———. *Hang on a Minute, Mate* (stories). Wellington: Reed, 1961.

———. *There and Back* (stories). Wellington: Reed, 1963.

Davin, Dan M. (b. 1913). *Breathing Spaces* (stories). London: R. Hale, 1975.

———. *Brides of Price.* London: R. Hale, 1972.

————. *For the Rest of Our Lives.* London: Nicholson, 1947. Reprint. London: Joseph, 1965; Auckland: Paul, 1965.

————. *The Gorse Blooms Pale* (stories). London: Nicholson, 1947.

————. *No Remittance.* London: Joseph, 1959.

————. *Not Here, Not Now.* London: R. Hale, 1970.

————. *Roads from Home.* London: Joseph, 1949. Reprint. Introduction by L. Jones. Auckland: Auckland University Press and Oxford University Press, 1976.

————. *The Sullen Bell.* London: Joseph, 1956. [H. Winston Rhodes, "Dan Davin's *Roads from Home,*" in *Critical Essays on the New Zealand Novel,* ed. Cherry Hankin (Auckland: Heinemann, 1976), pp. 73–87.]

Devanny, Jean (1894–1962). *Bushman Burke.* London: Duckworth, 1930.

————. *The Butcher Shop.* London: Duckworth, 1926.

————. *Dawn Beloved.* London: Duckworth, 1928.

————. *Lenore Divine.* London: Duckworth, 1927.

————. *Old Savage, and Other Stories.* London: Duckworth, 1927.

Duckworth, Marilyn (b. 1935). *A Barbarous Tongue.* London: Hutchinson, 1963.

————. *A Gap in the Spectrum.* London: New Authors, 1958.

————. *The Matchbox House.* London: Hutchinson, 1960.

————. *Over the Fence Is Out.* London: Hutchinson, 1969.

Du Fresne, Yvonne (b. 1929). *Farvel and Other Stories.* Wellington: Victoria University Press and Price Milburn, 1980.

Duggan, Maurice (1922–1974). *Collected Stories.* Edited by C. K. Stead. Auckland: Auckland University Press and Oxford University Press, 1981.

————. *Immanuel's Land.* Auckland: Pilgrim, 1957.

————. *O'Leary's Orchard and Other Stories.* Christchurch: Caxton, 1970.

————. *Summer in the Gravel Pit* (stories). London: Gollancz, 1965. [Patrick Evans, "Maurice Duggan and the Provincial Dilemma," *Landfall* 36 (June 1982):217–30; Bill Pearson, "A Self-Exacting Writer," in *Fretful Sleepers and Other Essays* (Auckland and London: Heinemann, 1974), pp. 43–45.]

Escott, Margaret [C. M. Allen] (b. 1908). *Show Down.* Edited and with an introduction by Robert Chapman. Auckland: Auckland University Press and Oxford University Press, 1973 [1936].

Ferguson, Dugald (1833–1920). *Bush Life.* London: Swan, 1893.

Finlayson, Roderick (b. 1904). *Brown Man's Burden* (stories). Edited and with an introduction by Bill Pearson. Auckland: Auckland University Press and Oxford University Press, 1973 [1938].

————. *Other Lovers* (three tales). Dunedin: McIndoe, 1976.

————. *The Schooner Came to Atia.* Auckland: Griffin, 1953.

————. *Sweet Beulah Land* (stories). Auckland: Griffin, 1942.

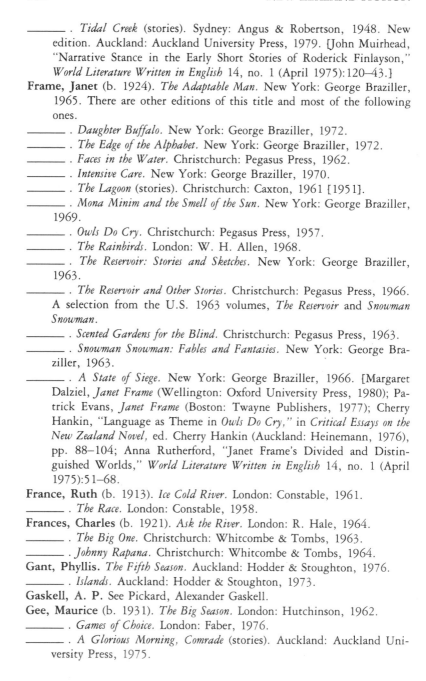

_____. *Tidal Creek* (stories). Sydney: Angus & Robertson, 1948. New edition. Auckland: Auckland University Press, 1979. [John Muirhead, "Narrative Stance in the Early Short Stories of Roderick Finlayson," *World Literature Written in English* 14, no. 1 (April 1975):120–43.]

Frame, Janet (b. 1924). *The Adaptable Man.* New York: George Braziller, 1965. There are other editions of this title and most of the following ones.

_____. *Daughter Buffalo.* New York: George Braziller, 1972.

_____. *The Edge of the Alphabet.* New York: George Braziller, 1972.

_____. *Faces in the Water.* Christchurch: Pegasus Press, 1962.

_____. *Intensive Care.* New York: George Braziller, 1970.

_____. *The Lagoon* (stories). Christchurch: Caxton, 1961 [1951].

_____. *Mona Minim and the Smell of the Sun.* New York: George Braziller, 1969.

_____. *Owls Do Cry.* Christchurch: Pegasus Press, 1957.

_____. *The Rainbirds.* London: W. H. Allen, 1968.

_____. *The Reservoir: Stories and Sketches.* New York: George Braziller, 1963.

_____. *The Reservoir and Other Stories.* Christchurch: Pegasus Press, 1966. A selection from the U.S. 1963 volumes, *The Reservoir* and *Snowman Snowman.*

_____. *Scented Gardens for the Blind.* Christchurch: Pegasus Press, 1963.

_____. *Snowman Snowman: Fables and Fantasies.* New York: George Braziller, 1963.

_____. *A State of Siege.* New York: George Braziller, 1966. [Margaret Dalziel, *Janet Frame* (Wellington: Oxford University Press, 1980); Patrick Evans, *Janet Frame* (Boston: Twayne Publishers, 1977); Cherry Hankin, "Language as Theme in *Owls Do Cry,*" in *Critical Essays on the New Zealand Novel,* ed. Cherry Hankin (Auckland: Heinemann, 1976), pp. 88–104; Anna Rutherford, "Janet Frame's Divided and Distinguished Worlds," *World Literature Written in English* 14, no. 1 (April 1975):51–68.

France, Ruth (b. 1913). *Ice Cold River.* London: Constable, 1961.

_____. *The Race.* London: Constable, 1958.

Frances, Charles (b. 1921). *Ask the River.* London: R. Hale, 1964.

_____. *The Big One.* Christchurch: Whitcombe & Tombs, 1963.

_____. *Johnny Rapana.* Christchurch: Whitcombe & Tombs, 1964.

Gant, Phyllis. *The Fifth Season.* Auckland: Hodder & Stoughton, 1976.

_____. *Islands.* Auckland: Hodder & Stoughton, 1973.

Gaskell, A. P. See Pickard, Alexander Gaskell.

Gee, Maurice (b. 1931). *The Big Season.* London: Hutchinson, 1962.

_____. *Games of Choice.* London: Faber, 1976.

_____. *A Glorious Morning, Comrade* (stories). Auckland: Auckland University Press, 1975.

———. *In My Father's Den*. London: Faber, 1972.

———. *Meg*. London: Faber, 1981.

———. *Plumb*. Sydney: Angus & Robertson, 1981 [1978].

———. *A Special Flower*. London: Hutchinson, 1965.

Gibson, Colin. *The Love-Keeper*. London: Chatto & Windus, 1970.

———. *The Pepper Leaf*. London: Chatto & Windus, 1971.

Gilbert, Gavin Robert (b. 1917). *Free to Laugh and Dance* (stories). Christchurch: Caxton, 1942.

———. *Glass Sharp and Poisonous*. Christchurch: Caxton, 1952.

———. *Love in a Lighthouse*. Christchurch: Pegasus, 1956.

Gillies, John Russell (b. 1920). *Voyagers in Aspic*. London: Collins, 1954.

Grace, Alfred A. (1867–1942). *Tales of a Dying Race*. London: Chatto & Windus, 1901.

Grace, Patricia (b. 1937). *The Dream Sleepers and Other Stories*. Auckland: Longman Paul, 1980.

———. *Mutuwhenua*. Auckland: Longman Paul, 1978.

———. *Waiariki* (stories). Auckland: Longman Paul, 1975.

Grossmann, Edith Searle (1863–1931). *The Heart of the Bush*. London: Sands, 1910.

Grover, Ray (b. 1931). *Another Man's Role*. Auckland: Paul, 1967.

Guthrie, John. See Brodie, John.

Hall, Sandi. *The Godmothers*. London: Women's Press, 1982.

Harlow, Michael. *Nothing but Switzerland and Lemonade*. Eastbourne, N.Z.: Hawk Press, 1980.

Harrison, Craig (b. 1914). *Broken October: New Zealand 1985*. Wellington: Reed, 1976.

Harvey, Norman B. *Any Old Dollars, Mister?* Auckland: Paul's Book Arcade, 1964.

Henderson, James Herbert (b. 1918). *Gunner Inglorious*. Christchurch: Whitcombe & Tombs, 1974 [1945].

Henderson, Michael (b. 1942). *The Log of a Superfluous Man*. Dunedin: McIndoe, 1975.

Henderson, Sylvia Constance [Sylvia Ashton-Warner] (b. 1908). *Bell Call*. New York: Simon & Schuster, 1964.

———. *Greenstone*. New York: Simon & Schuster, 1966.

———. *Incense to Idols*. London: Secker & Warburg, 1960.

———. *Spinster*. London: Virago Press, 1980 [1958].

———. *Three*. New York: Knopf, 1970.

Hilliard, Noel (b. 1929). *The Glory and the Dream*. Auckland: Heinemann, 1978.

———. *Maori Girl*. Auckland: Heinemann, 1971 [1960].

———. *Maori Woman*. Christchurch: Whitcombe & Tombs, 1974.

———. *A Night at Green River*. Christchurch: Whitcombe & Tombs, 1969; London: R. Hale, 1969.

————. *A Piece of Land* (stories). Christchurch: Whitcombe & Tombs, 1963; London: R. Hale, 1963.

————. *Power of Joy*. London: Joseph, 1965.

————. *Selected Stories*. Dunedin: McIndoe, 1977.

————. *Send Somebody Nice* (stories). London: R. Hale, 1976. [Bill Pearson, "A Parable of Exploitation," in *Fretful Sleepers and Other Essays* (Auckland and London: Heinemann, 1974), pp. 94–99.]

Holden, Anne (b. 1928). *The Empty Hills*. Christchurch: Whitcombe & Tombs, 1967.

————. *Rata*. Christchurch: Whitcombe & Tombs, 1965.

Hooker, John (b. 1932). *Jacob's Season*. London: Barrie & Jenkins, 1971.

Hooper, Peter. *The Goat Paddock and Other Stories*. Dunedin: McIndoe, 1981.

————. *A Song in the Forest*. Dunedin: McIndoe, 1979.

Hyde, Robin. See Wilkinson, Iris Guiver.

Ihimaera, Witi (b. 1944). *The New Net Goes Fishing* (stories). Auckland: Heinemann, 1977.

————. *Pounamu, Pounamu* (stories). Auckland: Heinemann, 1972.

————. *Tangi*. Auckland: Heinemann, 1973.

————. *Whanau*. Auckland: Heinemann, 1975. [John B. Beston, "An Interview with Witi Ihimaera," *World Literature Written in English* 16, no. 1 (April 1977):115–25; Witi Ihimaera, "Why I Write," *World Literature Written in English* 16, no. 1 (April 1977):117–19; Bill Pearson, "Recent Maori Writers," in *Fretful Sleepers and Other Essays* (Auckland and London: Heinemann, 1974), pp. 155–58.]

Jeffery, Margaret. *The Black Shore*. London: Heinemann, 1980.

————. *Cabin at Your Gate*. Wellington: Reed, 1973.

Joseph, George (b. 1912). *When the Rainbow Is Pale*. London: R. Hale, 1962.

Joseph, Michael Kennedy (b. 1914). *The Hole in the Zero*. New York: E. P. Dutton, 1968.

————. *I'll Soldier No More*. London: Gollancz, 1958; Hamilton, N.Z.: Paul, 1958.

————. *A Pound of Saffron*. London: Gollancz, 1962; Hamilton, N.Z.: Paul, 1962.

————. *A Soldier's Tale*. Auckland: Collins, 1977.

————. *The Time of Achamoen*. Auckland: Collins, 1977. [Bill Pearson, "M. K. Joseph's War Novel," in *Fretful Sleepers and Other Essays* (Auckland and London: Heinemann, 1974), pp. 80–84.]

Kalman, Yvonne. *Greenstone Land*. London: Macdonald, 1981.

Keinzly, Frances (b. 1922). *Tangahano*. London: Davies, 1960.

Kidman, Fiona (b. 1940). *A Breed of Women*. New York: Harper & Row, 1981.

————. *Mandarin Summer.* Auckland: Heinemann, 1981. [Interview in *Landfall* 34 (December 1980):352–61.]

Lee, John A. (b. 1891). *Children of the Poor.* London: W. Laurie, 1934.

————. *Civilian into Soldier.* London: W. Laurie, 1937.

————. *The Hunted.* Wellington: Price Milburn, 1975 [1936].

————. *Shiner Slattery.* Auckland: Collins, 1964.

————. *Soldier.* Auckland: Reed, 1977. [Dennis McEldowney, "John A. Lee's *Children of the Poor*," in *Critical Essays on the New Zealand Novel,* ed. Cherry Hankin (Auckland: Heinemann, 1976), pp. 24–39; John A. Lee, *The John A. Lee Diaries 1936–40* (Christchurch: Whitcoulls, 1981).]

McClenaghan, Jack (b. 1929). *Moving Target.* Wellington: Reed, 1966.

McDonald, Georgina (1905–1959). *Grand Hills for Sheep.* Christchurch: Whitcombe & Tombs, 1949.

————. *Stinson's Bush.* Christchurch: Whitcombe & Tombs, 1954.

McKenney, Kenneth (b. 1929). *The Hide-Away Man.* London: Barrie & Rockliff, 1965.

————. *The Orderly.* London: Deutsch, 1970.

————. *The Plants.* New York: Putnam, 1976.

McLeod, Catherine. *Fortunately There Was a Haystack.* Wellington: Reed, 1970.

McNeish, James (b. 1931). *The Glass Zoo.* London: Hodder & Stoughton, 1976.

————. *Mackenzie.* London: Hodder & Stoughton, 1970. [H. Winston Rhodes, "On Realising Fiction," *Landfall* 30 (September 1976):208–11.]

Maddock, Shirley (b. 1932). *With Gently Smiling Jaws.* Auckland: Collins, 1963.

Mander, Jane (1877–1949). *Allen Adair.* Edited and with an introduction by Dorothea Turner. Auckland: Auckland University Press and Oxford University Press, 1971 [1925].

————. *The Besieging City.* London: Hutchinson, 1926.

————. *The Passionate Puritan.* London: Lane, 1922.

————. *Pins and Pinnacles.* London: Hutchinson, 1928.

————. *The Story of a New Zealand River.* Christchurch: Whitcombe & Tombs, 1973 [1920].

————. *The Strange Attraction.* London: Lane, 1923. [Dorothea Turner, *Jane Mander* (New York: Twayne Publishers, 1972); Dorothea Turner, "*The Story of a New Zealand River*: Perceptions in an Unfixed Society," in *Critical Essays on the New Zealand Novel,* ed. Cherry Hankin (Auckland: Heinemann, 1976), pp. 1–23.]

Maning, Frederick E. (1811–1883).. *Old New Zealand.* Christchurch: Whitcombe & Tombs, n.d. [1963].

Mansfield, Katherine. See Murry, Kathleen Beauchamp.

Marsh, Ngaio (1899–1982). *Colour Scheme.* Boston: Little, Brown, 1943.

———. *Died in the Wool.* London: Collins, 1945.

———. *Vintage Murder.* London: G. Bles, 1937. [Ngaio March, *Black Beech and Honeydew: An Autobiography* (London: Collins, 1966).]

Mason, Henrietta. *Fool's Gold.* London: R. Hale, 1960.

Maughan, William. *Good and Faithful Servants.* Whatamongo Bay: Cape Catley, 1976 [1974].

Middleton, O. E. (b. 1925). *Confessions of an Ocelot and Not for a Seagull* (stories). Dunedin: McIndoe, 1979.

———. *The Loners* (stories). Dunedin: Square & Circle, 1972.

———. *Selected Stories.* Dunedin: McIndoe, 1976.

———. *The Stone and Other Stories.* Auckland: Pilgrim Press, 1959.

———. *A Walk on the Beach* (stories). London: M. Joseph, 1964. [Bill Pearson, "O. E. Middleton's Stories," in *Fretful Sleepers and Other Essays* (Auckland and London: Heinemann, 1974), pp. 72–74.]

Mincher, Philip. *The Ride Home: A Story Sequence.* Auckland: Longman Paul, 1977.

Mitcalfe, Barry (b. 1930). *I Say, Wait for Me* (stories). Hamilton, N.Z.: Outrigger, 1976.

———. *Moana.* Wellington: Sevenseas, 1975.

———. *Salvation Jones* (stories). Auckland: Mate Books, 1962.

Morrieson, Ronald Hugh (1922–1972). *Came a Hot Friday.* Sydney: Angus & Robertson, 1964.

———. *Pallet on the Floor.* Palmerston North, N.Z.: Dunmore Press, 1976.

———. *Predicament.* Palmerston North, N.Z.: Dunmore Press, 1974.

———. *The Scarecrow.* London: Angus & Robertson, 1964. Reprint. Auckland: Heinemann, 1976. [Maurice Shadbolt, Introduction to *Predicament* (Palmerston North, N.Z.: Dunmore Press, 1974); Peter Simpson, *Ronald Hugh Morrieson* (Auckland: Oxford, 1982).]

Muir, Robin (b. 1918). *Word for Word.* Christchurch: Pegasus, 1960.

Mulcock, Anne. *Landscape with Figures.* London: R. Hale, 1971.

Mulgan, Alan (1881–1962). *Spur of the Morning.* London: Dent, 1934.

Mulgan, John (1911–1945). *Man Alone.* London: Selwyn, 1939. Other editions are available. [Paul W. Day, *John Mulgan* (New York: Twayne Publishers, 1968); Paul W. Day, "Mulgan's *Man Alone*," in *Critical Essays on the New Zealand Novel,* ed. Cherry Hankin (Auckland: Heinemann, 1976), pp. 60–72.]

Murry, Kathleen Beauchamp [Katherine Mansfield] (1888–1923). *Collected Stories.* London: Constable, 1945.

———. *Complete Stories.* Auckland: Golden Press and Whitcombe & Tombs, 1974.

————. *Selected Short Stories.* Edited by Dan Davin. London: Oxford University Press, 1953.

————. *34 Short Stories.* Selected with an introduction by Elizabeth Bowen. London: Collins, 1957.

————. *Undiscovered Country: The New Zealand Stories of Katherine Mansfield.* Edited by Ian Gordon. London: Longman, 1974. [Antony Alpers, *The Life of Katherine Mansfield* (New York: Viking, 1980); Saralyn R. Daly, *Katherine Mansfield* (New York: Twayne Publishers, 1965); Ian Gordon, *Katherine Mansfield,* rev. ed. (London: Longman, 1971).]

O'Sullivan, Vincent (b. 1937). *The Boy, the Bridge, the River.* Dunedin: McIndoe, 1978.

————. *Miracle.* Dunedin: McIndoe, 1976.

Park, Ruth (b. 1923). *The Frost and the Fire.* Boston: Houghton Mifflin, 1958.

————. *One-a-Pecker, Two-a-Pecker.* Sydney: Angus & Robertson, 1957.

————. *The Witch's Thorn.* Sydney: Angus & Robertson, 1951.

Pearson, Bill (b. 1922). *Coal Flat.* Auckland: Heinemann, 1976 [1963]. [Allen Curnow, "*Coal Flat* Revisited," in *Critical Essays on the New Zealand Novel,* ed. Cherry Hankin (Auckland: Heinemann, 1976), pp. 105–27.]

Pickard, Alexander Gaskell [A. P. Gaskell] (b. 1913). *The Big Game and Other Stories.* Christchurch: Caxton, 1947. Expanded edition, *All Part of the Game and Other Stories.* Introduction by R. A. Copland. Auckland: Auckland University Press, 1978.

Sargeson, Frank (1903–1982). *Collected Stories.* Introduction by Bill Pearson. Hamilton, N.Z.: Paul, 1964.

————. *Conversation with My Uncle.* Auckland: Unicorn, 1936.

————. *En Route.* Wellington: Reed, 1979.

————. *The Hangover.* London: MacGibbon & Kee, 1967.

————. *I for One.* Christchurch: Caxton, 1954.

————. *I Saw in My Dream.* London: John Lehmann, 1949. Reprint. Introduction by H. W. Rhodes. Auckland: Auckland University Press and Oxford University Press, 1974.

————. *Joy of the Worm.* London: MacGibbon & Kee, 1969.

————. *A Man and His Wife* (stories). Christchurch: Caxton, 1940.

————. *Man of England Now.* London: Martin Brian & O'Keeffe, 1972.

————. *Memoirs of a Peon.* London: MacGibbon & Kee, 1965. Reprint. Auckland: Heinemann, 1974.

————. *The Stories of Frank Sargeson.* Auckland: Penguin, 1982 [1973].

————. *Sunset Village.* London: Martin Brian & O'Keeffe, 1976.

————. *That Summer and Other Stories.* London: John Lehmann, 1946.

————. *When the Wind Blows* (stories). Christchurch: Caxton, 1945. [R. A. Copland, "Frank Sargeson: *Memoirs of a Peon*," in *Critical Essays on the New Zealand Novel,* ed. Cherry Hankin (Auckland: Heinemann, 1976), pp. 128–39; Helen L. Hofman, ed., *The Puritan and the Waif: Critical Essays on the Work of Frank Sargeson* (Auckland: published by the editor, 1954); *Islands* 6, no. 3 (March 1978), special all-Sargeson number; Dennis McEldowney, *Frank Sargeson in His Time* (Dunedin, N.Z.: McIndoe, 1976); W. H. New, "Enclosures: Frank Sargeson's *I Saw in My Dream,*" *World Literature Written in English* 14, no. 1 (April 1975):15–23; H. Winston Rhodes, *Frank Sargeson* (New York: Twayne Publishers, 1969).]

Satchell, William (1860–1942). *The Elixir of Life.* London: Chapman & Hall, 1907.

————. *The Greenstone Door.* Auckland: Golden Press, 1973 [1914].

————. *The Land of the Lost.* Introduction by K. Smithyman. Auckland: Auckland University Press and Oxford University Press, 1971 [1902].

————. *The Toll of the Bush.* London: Macmillan, 1905. [Phillip Wilson, *William Satchell* (New York: Twayne Publishers, 1968).]

Scanlan, Nelle M. (1882–1968). *Pencarrow.* London: Jarrolds, 1932. [Nelle Scanlan, *Road to Pencarrow* (London: Hale, 1963).]

Scott, Mary (1888–1979). *Breakfast at Six.* London: Arrow Books, 1965.

————. *One of the Family.* Sydney: Angus & Robertson, 1958.

————. *The Unwritten Book.* London: H. Jenkins, 1957.

Scrimgeour, G. J. (b. 1934). *A Woman of Her Times.* London: M. Joseph, 1982.

Shadbolt, Maurice (b. 1932). *Among the Cinders.* Christchurch: Whitcombe & Tombs, 1975 [1965].

————. *Danger Zone.* London: Hodder & Stoughton, 1976.

————. *An Ear of the Dragon.* London: Cassell, 1971.

————. *Figures in Light: Selected Stories.* London: Hodder & Stoughton, 1978.

————. *The Lovelock Version.* Auckland: Hodder & Stoughton, 1980.

————. *The New Zealanders* (stories). Christchurch: Whitcombe & Tombs, 1974 [1959].

————. *The Presence of Music: Three Novellas.* London: Cassell, 1967.

————. *Strangers and Journeys.* London: Hodder & Stoughton, 1972.

————. *Summer Fires and Winter Country* (stories). London: Eyre & Spottiswoode, 1963.

————. *This Summer's Dolphin.* London: Cassell, 1969.

————. *A Touch of Clay.* London: Hodder & Stoughton, 1974. [Lawrence Jones, "Ambition and Accomplishment in Maurice Shadbolt's *Strangers and Journeys,*" in *Critical Essays on the New Zealand Novel,* ed. Cherry Hankin (Auckland: Heinemann, 1976), pp. 140–68; Bill Pearson, "A Mixed Peformance," in *Fretful Sleepers and Other Essays* (Auckland and London: Heinemann, 1974), pp. 75–79.]

Shaw, Helen (b. 1913). *The Gipsies and Other Stories.* Wellington: Victoria University Press and Price Milburn, 1978.

————. *The Orange Tree* (stories). Auckland: Pelorus, 1957.
Simons, **Wendy**. *Harper's Mother*. London: Angus & Robertson, 1980.
————. *Odd Woman Out*. Sydney: Angus & Robertson, 1980.
Slatter, **Gordon C.** (b. 1922). *A Gun in My Hand*. Christchurch: Pegasus, 1959.
Sligo, **John**. *The Cave*. Dunedin, N.Z.: McIndoe, 1978.
Stead, **C. K.** (b. 1932). *Smith's Dream*. New York: International Publications Service, 1974.
Stoney, **Henry Butler** (1816–1894). *Taranaki: A Tale of the War*. Auckland: W. C. Wilson, 1861.
Sutherland, **Margaret** (b. 1941). *The Fledgling*. London: Heinemann, 1974.
————. *Getting Through and Other Stories*. London: Heinemann, 1977.
————. *The Love Contract*. Auckland: Heinemann, 1976.
Sweven, **Godfrey**. See Brown, J. Macmillan.
Taylor, **William** (b. 1940). *The Persimmon Tree*. London: R. Hale, 1972.
Thompson, **Nola D.** (b. 1927). *The Sharemilkers*. Auckland: Paul, 1966.
Tregear, **Edward** (1846–1931). *Hedged with Divinities*. Wellington: R. Coupland Harding, 1895.
Vogel, **Harry B.** (1868–1947). *A Maori Maid*. London: Pearson, 1898.
Vogel, **Julius** (1835–1899). *Anno Domini 2000; or, Woman's Destiny*. London: Hutchinson, 1889.
Watson, **Jean**. *The Balloon Watchers*. Palmerston North, N.Z.: Dunmore Press, 1975.
————. *Stand in the Rain*. Indianapolis: Bobbs-Merrill, 1966.
————. *The World Is an Orange and the Sun*. Palmerston North, N.Z.: Dunmore Press, 1978.
Webb, **Alice F.** (1876–1963). *Miss Peter's Special and Other Stories*. London: Allenson, 1926.
Wedde, **Ian** (b. 1946). *Dick Seddon's Great Dive*. *Islands* 6 (November 1976):117–212. Entire issue.
Wendt, **Albert** (b. 1939). *Flying-Fox in a Freedom Tree* (stories). Auckland: Longman Paul, 1974.
————. *Leaves of the Banyan Tree*. Auckland: Longman Paul, 1979.
————. *Pouliuli* (stories). Auckland: Longman Paul, 1977.
————. *Sons for the Return Home*. Auckland: Longman Paul, 1973. [John B. Beston and Rose Marie Beston, "An Interview with Albert Wendt," *World Literature Written in English* 16, no. 1 (April 1977):151–62; Roger Robinson, "Albert Wendt: An Assessment," *Landfall* 34 (September 1980):275–89.]
Weston, **Jessie Edith** (1867–1944). *Ko Meri*. London: Eden Remington & Co., 1890.
White, **John** (1826–1891). *Te Rou; or, the Maori at Home*. London: Sampson, Low, 1874.
Wilkinson, **Iris Guiver** {Robin Hyde} (1906–1939). *Check to Your King*. London: Hurst & Blackett, 1936.

————. *The Godwits Fly.* Edited and with an introduction by Gloria Rawlinson. Auckland: Auckland University Press and Oxford University Press, 1970 [1937].

————. *Nor the Years Condemn.* London: Hurst & Blackett, 1938.

————. *Passport to Hell.* London: Hurst & Blackett, 1937.

————. *Wednesday's Children.* London: Hurst & Blackett, 1937. [James Bertram, "Robin Hyde: A Reassessment," *Landfall* 7 (September 1953):181–91; Frank Birbalsingh, "Robin Hyde," *Landfall* 31 (December 1977):362–76; Gloria Rawlinson, "Robin Hyde and *The Godwits Fly,*" in *Critical Essays on the New Zealand Novel,* ed. Cherry Hankin (Auckland: Heinemann, 1976), pp. 40–59.]

Wilson, George H. (1833–1905). *Ena, or the Ancient Maori.* London: Smith, Elder, 1874.

Wilson, Guthrie (b. 1914). *Brave Company.* London: Allen & Unwin, 1951.

————. *The Feared and the Fearless.* New York: Putnam, 1953.

————. *Julien Ware.* London: R. Hale, 1952.

————. *Sweet White Wine.* London: R. Hale, 1956.

Wilson, Phillip (b. 1922). *Beneath the Thunder.* Christchurch: Whitcombe & Tombs, 1963; London: R. Hale, 1963.

————. *New Zealand Jack.* London: R. Hale, 1973.

————. *The Outcasts.* London: R. Hale, 1965.

————. *Pacific Flight.* London: R. Hale, 1964.

————. *Some Are Lucky.* Wellington: Dennis Glover, 1960.

Young, Guy (1919–1957). *A Country Like Home* (sketches). Christchurch: Caxton, 1965.

Index